Bloom's
GUIDES

Jane Austen's
Pride and Prejudice

1984
The Adventures of Huckleberry Finn
All the Pretty Horses
Beloved
Brave New World
The Chosen
The Crucible
Cry, the Beloved Country
Death of a Salesman
The Grapes of Wrath
Great Expectations
Hamlet
The Handmaid's Tale
The House on Mango Street
I Know Why the Caged Bird Sings
The Iliad
Lord of the Flies
Macbeth
Maggie: A Girl of the Streets
The Member of the Wedding
Pride and Prejudice
Ragtime
Romeo and Juliet
The Scarlet Letter
Snow Falling on Cedars
A Streetcar Named Desire
The Things They Carried
To Kill a Mockingbird

Bloom's
GUIDES

Jane Austen's
Pride and Prejudice

Edited & with an Introduction
by Harold Bloom

CHELSEA HOUSE
P U B L I S H E R S
A Haights Cross Communications ✔ Company
Philadelphia

Introduction © 2005 by Harold Bloom.

Printed and bound in the United States of America.

First Printing
1 3 5 7 9 8 6 4 2

Library of Congress Cataloging-in-Publication Data

Jane Austen's Pride and Prejudice / Harold Bloom, ed.
    p. cm. — (Bloom's guides)
  Includes bibliographical references and index.
  ISBN 0-7910-8169-9 (alk. paper)
  1. Austen, Jane, 1775-1817. Pride and prejudice—Examinations—
Study guides. I. Bloom, Harold. II. Series.
  PR4034.P72J365 2004
  823'.7—dc22
                                        2004012659

Contributing editor: Bridget M. Marshall
Cover design by Takeshi Takahashi
Layout by EJB Publishing Services

Contents

# Introduction

HAROLD BLOOM

If the authentic test for a great novel is rereading, and the joys of yet further rereadings, then *Pride and Prejudice* can rival any novel ever written. Though Jane Austen, unlike Shakespeare, practices an art of rigorous exclusion, she seems to me finally the most Shakespearean novelist in the language. When Shakespeare wishes to, he can make all his personages, major and minor, speak in voices entirely their own, self-consistent and utterly different from one another. Austen, with the similar illusion of ease, does the same. Since voice in both writers is an image of personality and also of character, the reader of Austen encounters an astonishing variety of selves in her socially confined world. Though that world is essentially a secularized culture, the moral vision dominating it remains that of the Protestant sensibility. Austen's heroines waver in one judgment or another, but they hold fast to the right of private judgment as the self's fortress. What they call "affection" we term "love," of the enduring rather than the Romantic variety, and when they judge a man to be "amiable," it is akin to whatever superlative each of us may favor for an admirable, human person. Where they may differ from us, but more in degree than in kind, is in their profound reliance upon the soul's exchanges of mutual esteem with other souls. In *Pride and Prejudice* and *Emma* in particular, your accuracy in estimating the nature and value of another soul is intimately allied to the legitimacy of your self-esteem, your valid pride.

The moral comedy of the misunderstandings between Elizabeth Bennet and Darcy has been compared, by several critics, to the combat of wit between Beatrice and Benedick in Shakespeare's *Much Ado About Nothing*. As a comparison, this has limited usefulness: Elizabeth is not primarily a wit or a social ironist. Her true Shakespearean precursor is Rosalind in *As You Like It*. Rosalind resorts to furious wit in properly squelching Jacques and Touchstone, but her fundamental strength is a sure sense of self, with the wisdom that only an accurate self-estimate can bring. Such wisdom transcends detachment and welcomes a generous concern with other selves. It leads to a pride that is also playful, which is an intense contrast to Darcy's implacable pride. His sense of self relies upon an immense conviction of personal as well as societal eminence. We cannot dispute his conviction; he is intellectually formidable, morally fair-minded, and a better judge of character than Elizabeth sometimes proves to be. But his aggressiveness is excessive, despite Elizabeth's final, justified verdict: "He is frequently amiable." There is a touch of the quixotic in Elizabeth, while Darcy stands outside what could be termed the order of play. Tact without playfulness can yield too readily to moral zeal; but the quixotic not only can be tactless, it can decay into misguided exuberance.

Such reflections, though germane to *Pride and Prejudice*, are sadly abstract when applied to the lively comedy of the novel. Surprise keeps breaking in, and nothing turns out as anyone in the book expects. We are indeed in a Shakespearean world, as random in its way as Rosalind's Forest of Arden. Only the level firmness of Austen's narrative voice holds together a social world that borders oddly upon the bizarre, for everyone in it is rather more idiosyncratic than at first they appear to be. *Pride and Prejudice* has an authentic monster in Mr. Collins, a poseur in Wickham, a tyrant of pride in Lady Catherine, and a master of destructive satire in Mr. Bennet. There is a marvelous comic tension between Austen's seemingly normative tone and the eccentric personages who perpetually render the story more vivid and more strange.

Irony, which essentially is saying one thing while meaning another, is Austen's characteristic mode. Austen's irony, while endlessly genial, unsettles all her meanings. Where we seem most assured of the happiness or perfection attained by her heroines, we learn to look more closely and to surmise the implied reservations of this ironic vision. A great master of metaphor, Austen is also a genius of the unsaid: she expects the astute reader to say it for her. Not that Austen, in the manner of her Darcy, is a triumph of tact; she is more in the mode of her Elizabeth Bennet, and is a triumph of playfulness. In some ways, Austen is more like Shakespeare's Rosalind than Elizabeth ever could be, and so Austen's largest triumph is in the sheer psychic and spiritual health of her magnificent wit and invention.

Biographical Sketch

Most biographers of Jane Austen are quick to point out that she led a rather uneventful life. Indeed, she did not stray far from her birthplace, never married, and rarely stepped outside of the circle of her familial relationships. Nonetheless, her writing consistently conveys a keen observation of human behavior, particularly that of families and young women of her age in the middle and upper classes. Austen was born on December 16th 1775 in Steventon, Hampshire, in the south of England. She was the seventh of eight children of the Oxford-educated country parson, Rev. George Austen (1731–1805), and his wife, Cassandra (Leigh) Austen (1739–1827). Among Jane's siblings were six brothers, James (1765–1819), George (1766–1852), Edward (1767–1852), Henry (1771–1850), Frank (1774–1865) and Charles (1779–1852), and one sister, Cassandra Elizabeth (1773–1845). The two sisters were very close, as evidenced by the many letters from Jane to Cassandra that have survived. In 1785, Jane and Cassandra went to the Abbey boarding school in Reading. Other than this, the Austen girls had little formal education outside their family; however, this was not unusual for the times. Additionally, her father taught students at the rectory (Tomalin 261), and learning was highly valued in their household. Austen read copiously and widely, and she began writing as a very young woman. Austen's juvenilia, starting from the age of twelve, has been preserved and shows early indications of her major themes and her wise observations on the social life of her contemporaries. At only fourteen years of age, she wrote her first novel, *Love and Freindship* [sic] and a humorous history called *A History of England by a partial, prejudiced and ignorant Historian*. She also wrote plays that she and her sister performed for the family. Throughout her life, much of her work was read aloud to family members and friends. Her major literary influences included female writers of romantic novels, such as Fanny Burney, Maria Edgeworth, and Charlotte Smith.

Neither Austen girl ever married. Cassandra's fiancé Thomas Fowle died in 1797 of yellow fever contracted in the Caribbean, and she was never engaged again. Jane appears to have been involved in a few amorous relationships, and was once engaged for all of one day. In 1802, Austen received a proposal of marriage from Harris Bigg-Wither. She initially accepted, but the next day decided to revoke her acceptance. Other than this brief engagement, and a few romantic connections briefly mentioned in her correspondence, we have little record of Austen's love life.

Austen's family moved several times during her later life. Jane, Cassandra, and their parents moved from Stevenson to Bath in 1801. In 1805, her father died. In 1806 they moved from Bath to Clifton, and then to Southampton. Between 1801 and 1809, Austen did very little serious writing, leading many critics to suppose she was unhappy with her surroundings during this period. In 1809, she moved into a home provided by her brother Edward in Chawton, in Hampshire, not far from her childhood home; there she resumed writing more regularly. Later in this period, she became mildly ill, although she continued writing.

Austen completed *Persuasion* in 1816, despite her poor health. At this point, she was increasingly ill, and less able to write. In early 1817 she had to give up work on her final (and ultimately, unfinished) novel, *Sanditon*. Aware of the severity of her illness, now believed to be Addison's Disease, Austen made out her will on April 27th, leaving almost everything to her only sister, Cassandra. On May 24 she was moved to Winchester for medical treatment, but at the time, not much could be done for her. She died there on Friday, July 18th 1817, at the age of 41. Austen was buried in Winchester Cathedral on July 24th 1817.

Four of Austen's six novels, including *Sense and Sensibility* (1811), *Pride and Prejudice* (1813), *Mansfield Park* (1814), and *Emma* (1816), were published anonymously during her life-time. *Northanger Abbey* (written in 1798), and *Persuasion* (written in 1816), were published under her name a few months after her death. The initial inscription on her tomb made no mention of her career as an author. A brass tablet added at a later date by her nephew Mr. Austen-Leigh described her thus: "Jane Austen. Known to many by her writings, endeared to her family by the varied charms of her character and ennobled by her Christian faith and piety," and included the biblical quote "She openeth her mouth with wisdom and in her tongue is the law of kindness."

Works Cited

Tomalin, Claire. "Jane Austen's Childhood." *Pride and Prejudice: An Authoritative Text Backgrounds and Sources Criticism, Third Edition.* Ed. Donald Gray. New York: W.W. Norton & Company, 2001. 261–262.

The Story Behind the Story

Pride and Prejudice is considered to be Jane Austen's most popular novel. It is her most-translated novel, and has never gone out of print. *Pride and Prejudice* (and Jane Austen's work more generally) experienced a late twentieth-century revival in popularity in part due to film and television productions. A&E Networks and Britain's BBC commemorated the 200th anniversary of *Pride and Prejudice* (produced in 1995, it aired in the United States in 1996). The program proved widely popular in England and America, encouraging still more readers to Austen's most popular work.

Jane Austen began her writing career early; by age sixteen she had written several pieces for the entertainment of her family. She completed her first draft of a novel, *Elinor and Marianne*, in 1796; this would later become *Sense and Sensibility*. In her early publishing career, Austen repeatedly faced disappointment. In 1803 she sold *Northanger Abbey* (then titled *Susan*) to a publisher for ten pounds. However, the publisher chose not to print it, and only fourteen years later did *Northanger Abbey* actually appear in print. Unphased by the setback, Austen then revised *Sense and Sensibility*, which she would have published at her own risk in 1811. It appeared anonymously, merely establishing that it was "By a Lady." It received at least two fairly favorable reviews, and Austen eventually earned 140 pounds for the first edition.

The positive reception of *Sense and Sensibility* led to Austen's revisions of *First Impressions*, which would become *Pride and Prejudice*. Initially, Jane's father had sought a publisher for *First Impressions*, but it was rejected. In a letter to Martha Lloyd (later to be a wife of one of Austen's brothers), Austen wrote that she had hoped to get 150 pounds for the novel. (Gray, ed., 272) Eventually, she sold the copyright to it in November 1812 for the sum of 110 pounds to Thomas Egerton of London. While this conveniently provided her with immediate payment for her work, by selling her copyright she lost out on the profits of a second edition that was published later in 1813.

About 1,500 copies of the novel were published on January 29th, 1813. The title page of the text did not reveal Austen's authorship; rather, it read, "*Pride and Prejudice*: A novel. In three volumes. By the Author of *Sense and Sensibility*." Immediately quite popular, the edition sold out by July. Second editions of both *Pride and Prejudice* and *Sense and Sensibility* were published in November of 1813.

The title *Pride and Prejudice* came from a phrase in Francis Burney's 1782 novel *Cecilia*. In the final chapter of that novel, a character intones, "Yet this, however, remember; if to PRIDE AND PREJUDICE you owe your miseries, so wonderfully is good and evil balanced, that to PRIDE AND PREJUDICE you will also owe their termination" (930, capitalization in original). Austen was a reader of Burney's work, as well as a wide variety of other popular writers of the period. Her favorite writer, whom she often quotes in her novels, was Dr. Samuel Johnson (1709–1784). Johnson, one of the most quoted men of the 18th century, was a poet, essayist, and biographer. Among his many popular works, he published the *Dictionary of the English Language* in 1755, which became the definitive dictionary for the next 150 years, until the arrival of the Oxford English Dictionary. Like other writers of her period, Austen used this dictionary.

From all accounts, *Pride and Prejudice* was one of Austen's favorite pieces; in a letter to Cassandra written after she received the published copy of the novel, she wrote "I have got my own darling Child from London," referring to the novel. (Gray, ed., 273) Austen was particularly attached to the character of Elizabeth Bennet, of whom she wrote: "I must confess that *I* think her as delightful a character as ever appeared in print, and how I shall be able to tolerate those who do not like *her* at least, I do not know." (273) Despite her fondness for the novel, Austen was initially critical of it: "Upon the whole however I am quite vain enough & well satisfied enough.—The work is rather too light & bright & sparkling;—it wants shade;—it wants to be stretched out here & there" (273). Nonetheless, this novel is widely considered to be her best work.

In addition to its immediate popularity, *Pride and Prejudice* also received critical praise almost immediately. An anonymous reviewer in the *British Critic* in February of 1813 (one month after the novel's publication) wrote "It is very far superior to almost all the publications of the kind which have lately come before us. It has a very unexceptionable tendency, the story is well told, the characters remarkably well drawn and supported, and written with great spirit as well as vigour" (qtd. in Southam 41). The reviewer also comments on its accuracy: "The picture of the younger Miss Bennets, their perpetual visits to the market town where officers are quartered, and the result, is perhaps exemplified in every provincial town in the kingdom" (42). It closes with the sentiment that "It is unnecessary to add, that we have perused these volumes with much satisfaction and amusement, and entertain very little doubt that their successful circulation will induce the author to similar exertions" (42). A second review in March in the *Critical Review* claimed "We cannot conclude, without repeating our approbation of this performance, which rises very superior to any novel we have lately met with in the delineation of domestic scenes" (47). But despite its critical and popular success, Austen's authorship of the novel was kept a secret, even to some members of the family and close friends. In a playful letter, she describes reading the novel aloud to a friend: "Miss Benn dined with us on the very day of the Books coming, & in the even[ing] we set fairly at it & read half the [first volume] to her ... I believe it passed with her unsuspected.–She was amused, poor soul!"(Gray, ed., 273) *Pride and Prejudice* was Austen's greatest success, but one she seemed to enjoy best as a source of personal pride among close family and friends.

Works Cited
Burney, Frances. *Cecilia, or Memoirs of an Heiress*. Oxford: Oxford University Press, 1988.

Southam, B.C., Editor. *Jane Austen: The Critical Heritage. Revised Edition*. London: Routledge & Kegan Paul, 1986.

"To Martha Lloyd Sunday 29–Monday 30 November 1812." in *Pride and Prejudice: An Authoritative Text Backgrounds and Sources Criticism, Third*

Edition. Ed. Donald Gray. New York: W.W. Norton & Company, 2001: 272.

"To Cassandra Austen Friday 29 January 1813." *Pride and Prejudice: An Authoritative Text Backgrounds and Sources Criticism, Third Edition*. Ed. Donald Gray. New York: W.W. Norton & Company, 2001: 273.

"To Cassandra Austen Thursday 4 February." *Pride and Prejudice: An Authoritative Text Backgrounds and Sources Criticism, Third Edition*. Ed. Donald Gray. New York: W.W. Norton & Company, 2001: 273.

"To Cassandra Austen Friday 29 January 1813." *Pride and Prejudice: An Authoritative Text Backgrounds and Sources Criticism, Third Edition*. Ed. Donald Gray. New York: W.W. Norton & Company, 2001: 273.

List of Characters

Elizabeth Bennet is the novel's twenty-year-old protagonist and hero. She is the second of the five Bennet daughters, and the favorite of her father, since she is the most intelligent and sensible of the girls. She is the least favorite of Mrs. Bennet, who much prefers her prettier and livelier daughters. Elizabeth (also called "Lizzy") is courted first by Mr. Collins, then Mr. Wickham, then Mr. Darcy. She acquires an immediate dislike for Darcy, but eventually the two begin to understand one another, and they end happily married.

Mrs. Bennet has one goal in life: to get her daughters married well. Ironically, her obsessive pursuit of proper (read: wealthy) matches for her daughters nearly backfires, as potential suitors are repulsed by her behavior. The opening chapter establishes her as "a woman of mean understanding, little information, and uncertain temper" (3). The daughter of a Meryton attorney, she received a dowry of 4,000 pounds upon her marriage to Mr. Bennet.

Mr. Bennet, "an odd mixture of quick parts, sarcastic humor, and caprice" (3), is the patriarch of the Bennet family. His relationship with his wife is not one of equals; at best she amuses him, at worst annoys and disappoints him. He loves his daughters, particularly Elizabeth, but generally fails as a parent by refusing to educate or control their young instincts. Due to an entail, his estate will pass to the nearest male relative, Mr. Collins.

Jane Bennet, at twenty-two years of age, is the oldest and most beautiful Bennet daughter. She is often referred to as "Miss Bennet." A constant optimist, she finds it hard to think badly of anyone, even with a preponderance of evidence indicating the negative. Her lovely appearance and positive disposition are greatly prized by her mother, who expects her to make a good marriage. Jane falls in love with Mr. Bingley, a man well-suited to her in temperament; after a suitable season of separation and worry, the two marry happily.

Mary Bennet is the middle child of the Bennets. Studious and serious, she provides a foil to Lydia, the youngest daughter. Mary wishes to be known as "accomplished" rather than pretty, and enjoys displaying her musical skills at public events. Mary is unaware that her talents are less than she might wish, and her family is at times embarrassed by these performances. She is frequently moralizing and harshly judgmental at inappropriate times.

Catherine Bennet, also called Kitty, is the easily-influenced fourth Bennet sister. She is initially closely allied to Lydia, and the two are obsessed with the comings and goings of the officers of the local regiment. Later, she is influenced for the better by her older sisters in the absence of Lydia. She is good friends with Maria Lucas, who lives nearby.

Lydia Bennet is fifteen years old and the youngest Bennet sister. Immature and impetuous, she chases various soldiers and is a bad influence on her sister Kitty. She is Mrs. Bennet's favorite of the girls. Much to the concern of her older sisters, Lydia's impulsiveness remains unchecked. At sixteen, she elopes with Mr. Wickham and is nearly abandoned by him. She and the family are narrowly saved from serious embarrassment due to her behavior, but Lydia seems not to understand the depth of her plunge, and remains flighty, arrogant, and careless; she learns no real lesson from her brush with infamy.

Mr. Fitzwilliam Darcy is Mr. Bingley's best friend and the nephew of Lady Catherine de Bourgh. His aristocratic connections and considerable wealth make him a sought-after bachelor, but his excessive pride causes much consternation among the ladies of the area. A man of great pride, he is also honest and cautious. Despite initially insisting that there is not a pretty girl in all of Meryton, he eventually becomes attached to Elizabeth Bennet, to whom he makes a prideful, unromantic, (and rejected) proposal of marriage. Believing he merely speaks plainly, Darcy fails to see that his speeches often shock and anger his audiences. After realizing his haughty manner has been his downfall, Darcy learns humility, and eventually wins the hand of Elizabeth.

Mr. Bingley is the source of much neighborhood gossip when he moves to Netherfield, an estate neighboring Longbourne. Kind, generous, and easy-going, he immediately finds a like-minded soul in Jane, despite her family's class and social inferiority. He is best friends with Darcy, who steers him away from Jane, in part due to her poor connections. But Bingley cares little for money or status. With honest modesty, he believes that he has not won Jane's affection. Learning he has been deceived by his friend and sisters, he immediately returns to Jane to set things right, and also hastily forgives Darcy for his interference.

Mr. Collins is a cleric and a cousin to the Bennets. Mr. Collins visits their home with the intention of marrying one of the sisters, but the entire family finds him annoying and pompous, particularly in his attachment to his patroness, Lady Catherine de Bourgh. Collins is also the beneficiary of the entail on the Longbourne estate; when Mr. Bennet dies, he will receive it. Without any real affection, he proposes to Elizabeth, who rejects him outright in a very humorous scene in which Collins believes she is just playing coy. Despite his failure with Elizabeth, he does manage to land a wife—Charlotte Lucas—the very next day. His obsequious manner and absurd formality are repeatedly a source of humor in the novel.

Mr. George Wickham is a charming and handsome officer in the militia posted in Meryton. Elizabeth becomes interested in him, only to find that he soon moves on to another young woman who has recently come into an inheritance. He lies about his own history and that of Darcy, imputing Darcy's good name. It is later revealed that he attempted to seduce Darcy's sister Georgiana. He causes a great scandal by running off with

Lydia, presumably with no intention of marrying her. He is able to gain both money and position from Mr. Darcy, who intervenes on behalf of the Bennets. Wickham remains charming to the end, but also continues to be a gambler and money-waster. Wickham's behavior has been so insulting, that he is never allowed to visit Pemberley when Lydia comes to visit Elizabeth.

Caroline Bingley is Bingley's snobbish sister. Although she is fond of Jane, she merely tolerates Elizabeth, and scorns the rest of the Bennet family entirely. She attempts to win the affection of Darcy, but only succeeds in making Elizabeth that much more agreeable to him.

Louisa Bingley Hurst is Bingley's sister who is married to Mr. Hurst, "a man of more fashion than fortune" (10). She tends to share in Caroline's sentiments, but as a married sister, is somewhat removed from some of the politics of the situation.

Georgiana Darcy is Darcy's sister. The Bingley sisters claim to be quite fond of her, but it is possible that they are merely after the Darcy family connections, including both the money and the proximity to Georgiana's eligible brother Darcy. Darcy is very attached to his sister. She is known for having great musical talent. Darcy has gone to great lengths to protect his sister from rumors that she nearly eloped with and had her heart broken by the charming Wickham.

Lady Catherine de Bourgh is a wealthy upper-class woman with a large estate. She is the widow of Sir Lewis de Bourgh, and now lives at Rosings. She is used to getting her own way in everything, and is a most unpleasant woman. She is Mr. Collins' patron, and he idolizes her, though it is clear that she merely keeps him around to flatter her. She is also Darcy 's aunt, but he is less tolerant of her high airs.

Mr. Gardiner is Mrs. Bennet's brother. He is married and has four children with his wife. He and his wife are quite fond of the Bennet girls, particularly Elizabeth, and prove much better parents than the Bennets. It is Mr. Gardiner who works to recover Lydia in London, and the family believes that they are indebted to him for payments to Wickham to ensure their marriage.

Mrs. Gardiner is Mr. Gardiner's wife, and sister-in-law to Mrs. Bennet. A mother of four children (two girls and two boys), she is a sensible and observant woman, but knows how to keep her surmises to herself. She watches Mr. Darcy's behavior towards Elizabeth, and easily sees their attachment, but does nothing to reveal her knowledge or endanger the relationship. Elizabeth is quite attached to her.

Charlotte Lucas is Elizabeth's best friend, and is six years her senior. She is the oldest child (at 27) of the Lucases. When she receives and accepts a marriage proposal from Mr. Collins the day following his proposal to (and rejection by) Elizabeth, Elizabeth begins to question their friendship, and fears they will never be close again. Although Elizabeth does visit the Collins' home, she never feels the same closeness with Charlotte.

Colonel Forster is the commander of the militia regiment of which Wickham is a member. He is attentive and kind to the Bennet family after Lydia runs off with Wickham, and makes every attempt to find the two.

Mrs. Harriet Forster becomes a friend of Lydia while her husband's regiment is stationed at Meryton. She invites her to join them in Brighton, where Lydia runs off with Wickham.

Anne de Bourgh is Lady Catherine's daughter. She is quiet, sickly, and apparently snobbish.

Summary and Analysis*

The opening one-sentence paragraph of **Volume I, chapter 1**—"It is a truth universally acknowledged, that a single man in possession of a good fortune must be in want of a wife" (1)— goes far towards illustrating the tone of the narrative that follows. We are immediately plunged into a conversation occurring between Mr. and Mrs. Bennet, regarding a new arrival in the neighborhood. The fact that the Bennet household contains five single daughters makes that fact that the new arrival is rumored to be a single man of good fortune (who therefore must be in want of a wife), quite notable. The new arrival, named Mr. Bingley, is a subject of great importance to Mrs. Bennet, but of little interest to her husband. We also learn of other locals in the area, including Mrs. Long, who provided the initial rumor, Mr. Morris, who was involved in the procurement of the estate, and Sir William and Lady Lucas, who will be visiting Bingley, much to Mrs. Bennet's concern, as the Lucases have marriageable daughters as well. Mr. Bennet immediately makes clear his preference for daughter Lizzy, and Mrs. Bennet seems equally clear of her lack of favoritism for this girl, preferring Jane for her beauty and Lydia for her larks. Mrs. Bennet's character is summed up in the closing lines of the chapter: "*Her* mind was less difficult to develop. She was a woman of mean understanding, little information, and uncertain temper. When she was discontented, she fancied herself nervous. The business of her life was to get her daughters married; its solace was visiting and news" (3). Mrs. Bennet will not modulate far from this, and indeed, the opening discussion between the two sets the model for their future interactions; Mr. Bennet tolerates and is general amused by Mrs. Bennet, while Mrs. Bennet feels afflicted by her husband's lack of concern for gossip and disdain for local neighborhood politics.

---

* The summary and analysis is based on the Oxford World Classics edition of the text.

Chapter 2 opens by informing us that Mr. Bennet has indeed visited Mr. Bingley, although he has kept this information from the ladies. Mrs. Bennet frets over how her girls will ever be introduced to him, until he finally reveals that he has paid the visit, which brings great pleasure to Mrs. Bennet and leads Lydia to anticipate a forthcoming ball.

In **chapter 3**, the Bennet ladies attempt to gain information about Mr. Bingley from Mr. Bennet. Mr. Bingley politely returns the visit, but only sees Mr. Bennet, although the girls do manage to get a good look at him from an upstairs window. We learn that Mr. Bingley has heard of the girls and their great beauty, and is disappointed at not seeing them. Mrs. Bennet extends a dinner invitation, which Bingley cannot accept. But Bingley does arrive at the ball, along with his two sisters, Miss Bingley and Mrs. Hurst, the sister's husband (Mr. Hurst), and his friend Mr. Darcy. Mr. Bingley and Mr. Darcy prove a study in contrast. Mr. Bingley is described as "good-looking and gentlemanlike; he had a pleasant countenance, and easy, unaffected manners" (6). While Bingley dances every dance and makes himself amiable to every guest, Darcy refuses to dance with women other than Bingley's sisters, and is pronounced most disagreeable by everyone present. Elizabeth overhears him slight her, which doesn't seem to bother her much, as "she had a lively, playful disposition, which delighted in anything ridiculous" (8). Mr. Bingley dances twice with Jane, and all the Bennet women are pleased with the outcome of the evening. The chapter ends with the ladies returning home to tell Mr. Bennet of their conquests. He is little interested in their tales. Mrs. Bennet reports on both Jane's success with Bingley and the horrid behavior of Darcy.

Jane and Elizabeth discuss their evening in **chapter 4**; Jane confesses her admiration for Bingley. We learn more of Jane's disposition from the exchange between the two sisters. Jane is kind and generous, and always eager to think the best of everyone. Elizabeth claims that Jane likes "to take the good of everybody's character and make it still better, and say nothing of the bad" (10). We also learn the details of Mr. Bingley's fortune; he has inherited a hundred thousand pounds from his father, who had intended to purchase an estate, but died before he was able to do so. We learn of Bingley's relationships with his sisters, who both find Jane Bennet to be a sweet girl. Bingley has a very high regard for and close relationship with Darcy, who "was clever. He was at the same time haughty, reserved, and fastidious, and his manners, though well-bred, were not inviting" (11). When Bingley and Darcy discuss the ball, Bingley reports that he has thoroughly enjoyed himself, and that "he could not conceive an angel more beautiful" than Jane Bennet (11). Darcy, on the other hand, claims that he saw no beauty, no fashion, and very little that pleased or interested him.

The Lucas family is introduced in **chapter 5**. Sir William Lucas, known as "inoffensive, friendly, and obliging" (12), made his fortune as a trader in Meryton. The family lives in Lucas Lodge, not far from Longbourn. The Lucases have several children, the oldest of which is Charlotte, aged 27, who is a dear friend of Elizabeth. The Lucas ladies visit the Bennets to discuss the previous evening's ball. Mrs. Bennet again raises the point that Mr. Bingley chose to dance with Jane twice, and further abuses Mr. Darcy's character for his slight of Elizabeth. During this exchange, Mary expounds on the sin of pride, as well as on the difference between pride and vanity. Her comments are of little interest to the rest of the company, and Mary appears very pedantic and dull.

Chapter 6 revolves around the exchange of visits between the Bennets and the Bingleys. Miss Bingley and Mrs. Hurst particularly like Jane and Elizabeth, but find their mother intolerable and their younger sisters worthless. Jane is pleased by their courteous treatment of her; Elizabeth is annoyed by their haughty treatment of the rest of the family. Elizabeth and her friend Charlotte discuss the growing connection between Jane and Bingley. Meanwhile, Elizabeth is unaware that Mr. Darcy has begun to observe her with growing interest; she has no idea that "he began to wish to know more of her" (16). Mr. Darcy's attempts to observe and join conversations with Elizabeth are a source of annoyance to her. Meanwhile, she is mortified at her sister Mary's performance: "Mary had neither genius nor taste; and though vanity had given her application, it had given her likewise a pedantic air and conceited manner" (17). Sir Lucas attempts civilities with Darcy about the pleasures of dancing, but Darcy never dances, and haughtily intones that "every savage can dance" (18). Mr. Lucas mistakenly attempts to get Darcy to dance with Elizabeth, but the refusals on both sides make for an awkward moment. Miss Bingley approaches Darcy with the intent of belittling the party they are attending, but she miscalculates; Darcy does not join in her critique, and instead comments on Elizabeth's "fine eyes" (19). Miss Bingley abuses the character of the Bennet family (particularly Mrs. Bennet), but Darcy ignores her, although Miss Bingley is unaware of this.

Chapter 7 begins with an explanation of the economic situation of the Bennets. Mr. Bennet has an estate of two thousand pounds a year, which is entailed to male heirs. Since the Bennets are all daughters, upon Mr. Bennet's death, the estate will go to the nearest male heir, a Mr. Collins. The only other money in the family is the four thousand pounds given to Mrs. Bennet by her father, an attorney. Mrs. Bennet has a sister, married to Mr. Phillips, who lives in the town of Meryton, only a mile distant from Longbourn. A militia regiment is stationed in the town, and the younger girls suddenly have an extra incentive to visit their aunt. Catherine (who is usually called Kitty) and Lydia are particularly enamored of these military men. Jane is invited to Netherfield, which overjoys Mrs. Bennet, who manages it so that Jane must go on horseback, with the hope that bad weather will follow and Jane will have to stay overnight. Although this element of the plan is successful, it has the unfortunate side effect of making Jane take ill. The next morning, Elizabeth walks to Netherfield to see her sister. After a long walk, she arrives with a glowing complexion and a dirty petticoat, which shows her hardiness, but also seems somewhat inappropriate to the pampered Bingley girls. She is invited to stay until her sister is well enough to go home.

Chapter 8 accounts an entertaining evening of parlor play at Netherfield. While Jane is ill, Elizabeth dines and socializes with the Bingleys and Darcy. Darcy plainly admires her, making Miss Bingley jealous, as she wishes to marry him herself. Jane is still ill, so they decide to call a doctor the next morning. Jane is feeling better the next morning, when **chapter 9** opens. Mrs. Bennet arrives at Jane's request, and insists that Jane is far worse, and cannot possibly be moved without damage to her health. Of course, this is all part of her ploy to keep Jane at Netherfield for as long as possible. Mrs. Bennet continues to mortify Elizabeth, discussing with Darcy the advantages of country life over London city living. She lets Mr. Bingley know that she keeps servants so that her daughters do not have to do housework or cooking (unlike the Lucases). At this rather inappropriate moment, Lydia reminds Bingley that he promised to give a ball at Netherfield; he promises to set the date as soon as Jane is better. Lydia further embarrasses Elizabeth by referring to the pleasure of having the military men included.

During **chapter 10** Jane continues to recover at Netherfield, and Elizabeth stays to mind her sister. She also dines with the family and their guests, and is able to observe the behavior of Miss Bingley and Darcy. Miss Bingley, attempting to gain the attentions of Darcy, compliments him excessively on his letter writing, but her behavior only annoys him. She teases him about his attraction to Elizabeth, but her behavior once again only makes Elizabeth look more appealing to Darcy. Elizabeth notices Darcy's observation of her, but cannot account for it, as she believes that he dislikes her. But she is not bothered, as "she liked him too little to care for his approbation" (38). After they exchange comments about dancing, "Darcy had never been so bewitched by any woman as he was by her" (38). But this private revelation is tempered by the following statement: "He really believed, that were it not for the inferiority of her connections, he should be in some danger" (38). Although Darcy can admire Elizabeth, her family is never far from his mind, and prevents his true consideration of her as a proper match. The party goes for a walk in the garden, and Mrs. Hurst and Miss Bingley are openly rude to Elizabeth; Darcy attempts to make up for it, but before he can, Elizabeth gracefully and gleefully removes herself from their party, and joins Jane.

Jane is well enough to join the ladies in the parlor after dinner in **chapter 11**, and Elizabeth finds that they are all quite more agreeable in her presence, at least until the men arrive. But with the entrance of Darcy, Miss Bingley immediately turns her attention to him. Miss Bingley tells Elizabeth that Mr. Darcy cannot be laughed at, and Elizabeth finds this to be a great character flaw indeed. The three joke and parry about character flaws, and Darcy admits that his greatest weakness is a resentful temper and that he holds a grudge. Their playful talk is ended by Miss Bingley, who insists on musical entertainment for the group because she feels left out of the conversation.

Jane and Elizabeth are ready to return home at the start of **chapter 12**. Their mother makes efforts to keep them there by refusing to send the carriage, but the girls borrow Mr. Bingley's and are on their way. The Bingley sisters and Mr. Darcy are relieved to see them leave, though for different reasons. Miss Bingley is glad to be rid of her competition, but Darcy is simply glad to be spared further rudeness by Miss Bingley towards Elizabeth, who continues to "attract him more than he liked" (44). Mrs. Bennet is annoyed with their early return. Mary is engrossed in her music, while Catherine and Lydia talk only of the militia.

At the beginning of **chapter 13**, Mr. Bennet announces that they will receive a guest in the house, their cousin, Mr. Collins, who is also the man who will inherit the Longbourn estate. Mr. Collins' pompous letter is read aloud; in it he repeatedly refers to his relationship with his noble patron, Lady Catherine de Bourgh. He intends that his visit reunite him with the family (his father had a falling out with Mr. Bennet before his death). Mr. Collins, the rector of Lady de Bourgh's parish in Hunsford, is 25 years old, excessively formal and obsequious, and eager to show his connections with nobility. He informs the girls that he has come "prepared to admire them" (49); indicating that he intends to marry one of them so that the entire family may remain in the Longbourn estate. Although she does not dwell extensively on it, Austen portrays the serious limitations that the economic and social order of her society placed on women.

Lacking an inheritance, the Bennet women must marry well or face hardship. Their marrying well is further impaired by their lack of an inheritance.

Throughout **chapter 14**, Collins repeatedly praises his patroness, and his own good fortune in being so closely connected with her socially. He mentions her daughter, "the most charming young lady" (50) who is not in good health, which results in Lady de Bourgh staying home a great deal. The fact that Mr. Collins is an absurd character immediately makes us suspect his judgment of the de Bourghs, who we will not meet first-hand for several chapters. These descriptions prepare the Bennets and the reader for that future meeting. Mr. Bennet is completely amused by Mr. Collins' absurd talk, but he soon grows tired of him. Perhaps to be an annoyance to his daughters, he suggests that Mr. Collins read aloud to them. Mr. Collins reads from a series of sermons, much to the ladies' disappointment. Lydia ignores social custom, and rudely begins talking during the reading, putting an end to the annoyance for all of them. She is scolded for her behavior, but none of them are really sad to put an end to Collins' performance.

Mr. Collins hints in **chapter 15** that he is interested in Jane; Mrs. Bennet suggests that she is likely to be engaged to another (implying Bingley), so in his ever-practical way, Collins immediately moves on to the second daughter. Mr. Collins and the girls walk to Meryton to see their aunt, Mrs. Phillips, and on the way meet some of the militia officers, including Mr. Denny, who Lydia and Catherine already know. He introduces them to Mr. Wickham. Soon after their meeting, Bingley and Darcy arrive as well and explain that they had attempted to seek the ladies at Longbourn. Elizabeth watches as Darcy and Mr. Wickham see each other and change color; they seem barely able to exchange civilities. Darcy and Bingley hurry on. The girls and Mr. Collins relax at Mrs. Phillips' house, and she invites them to a party the following night.

In **chapter 16** the girls and Mr. Collins return to Mrs. Phillips' as promised. Upon their arrival, they learn that Mr. Wickham is there. Mr. Collins again goes on about Lady Catherine and her estate at Rosings; Mrs. Phillips is an engaged listener. Mr. Wickham is acknowledged by all as the most superior of men, and Elizabeth has the pleasure of receiving a great measure of his attentions for the evening. Wickham takes the opportunity to explain the awkward meeting between himself and Darcy, telling Elizabeth that Mr. Darcy has done him a grave ill by refusing to make good on a promise that Mr. Darcy's father made to Wickham. He claims that he was to join the clergy, but that he was unable to do so because of Mr. Darcy's refusal to give him the allowance promised by his father. Elizabeth is outraged, and wishes for Mr. Darcy to be publicly humiliated for his behavior; Mr. Wickham will not hear of it, but is relieved to hear that Elizabeth has found him prideful and rude, and that the general opinion of him in Meryton is not a positive one. He also claims that Miss Darcy is very proud and haughty like her brother. Wickham also explains the further connections of Darcy's family. Since Lady Catherine de Bourgh and now-deceased Lady Anne Darcy are sisters, Lady Catherine is Darcy's aunt, and it is rumored that Darcy and Lady Catherine's daughter were intended for one another, in order to join the families' two fortunes. Wickham confirms Elizabeth's suspicions that Lady Catherine is pompous and proud, and only gains her good reputation (that we have heard from Collins) through her wealth and power. Elizabeth is much impressed with Wickham, as are the other ladies of the company.

Elizabeth shares her gossip about Darcy with Jane at the opening of **chapter 17**, and Jane is astonished. Mr. Bingley and his sisters arrive to invite them to the ball at Netherfield for the following Tuesday, and the rest of the chapter involves the preparations for the event. Mr. Collins asks Elizabeth if she will dance with him at the ball, and "it now first struck her, that she was selected from among her sisters as worthy of being the mistress of Hunsford Parsonage" (67); this is not a thought that pleases her.

Chapter 18 opens at the much-anticipated ball. Elizabeth is disappointed to find that Wickham is not there, and further vexed to think that the reason is Mr. Darcy. The first two dances, which she has promised to Mr. Collins, are painful to her, and "the moment of her release from him was ecstasy" (68). She then dances with others, and learns that Wickham is "universally liked" (68), further endearing him to her. She is taken by surprise by an offer from Darcy to dance; the two make awkward conversation, and Elizabeth tells him "I have always seen a great similarity in the turn of our minds. We are each of an unsocial, taciturn disposition, unwilling to speak, unless we expect to say something that will amaze the whole room" (69). Although she means this as a compliment to neither, it does indeed point out a similarity between the two that will become a striking feature of their relationship. Elizabeth brings up Darcy's previous comment about being unforgiving, and the two discuss judgment; Elizabeth says "It is particularly incumbent on those who never change their opinion, to be secure of judging properly first" (71). This of course is a theme of the novel; Elizabeth wishes to have a clear judgment of him, but Darcy asks that she defer judgment for a time, to learn more of him. After their cold separation, Miss Bingley approaches Elizabeth, saying she has heard from her sister that she is enamored of George Wickham. She warns Elizabeth about him, telling her that he was the son of Mr. Darcy's steward, and warns her "not to give implicit confidence to all his assertions; for as to Mr. Darcy's using him ill, it is perfectly false" (72). Elizabeth does not take the information kindly, and Miss Bingley turns away sneering. Mr. Collins approaches Elizabeth with his exciting news: he has just learned that a nephew of Lady Catherine is present (meaning Darcy). He intends to introduce himself, a great breech of etiquette; Elizabeth attempts to dissuade him, but he explains that his position in the clergy entitles him to such an act (it doesn't). Elizabeth watches from afar, and sees the awkwardness of it all; Mr. Collins is oblivious and returns thinking he has been triumphant. Mrs. Bennet has been talking loudly and freely to Mrs. Lucas of her belief that Jane will soon be engaged to Mr. Bingley. Elizabeth is mortified, and begs her to stop, if only to avoid the notice of Mr. Darcy. Mary has been singing, and Elizabeth also wishes this would stop; her father intervenes to ask her to allow another girl to sing. Mr. Collins goes on about his duties as clergy. Elizabeth is completely mortified by the behavior of every member of her family, and particularly perturbed by the constant presence of Mr. Collins at her side. Mrs. Bennet once again manages to delay her carriage so that the Bennets are the last to leave the hall, and they have clearly overstayed their welcome. At the end of the chapter, Mrs. Bennet fully believes that her daughter Jane will be married to Bingley and Elizabeth will be married to Collins; she feels these are appropriate matches for each daughter.

Chapter 19 opens with Mr. Collins' startling proposal of marriage to Elizabeth. When Mr. Collins requests a private audience with her, Elizabeth begs her sisters to stay, but Mrs. Bennet makes a great show of removing them all. Mr. Collins' proposal is perhaps one of the most comical scenes in the novel. He explains his reasons for marrying, and for selecting Elizabeth, none of which have anything at all to do with her personal qualities. Elizabeth repeatedly makes her refusal clear, but Mr. Collins refuses to accept; he believes she is merely playing games, and claims that her refusals only make her more agreeable to him. Becoming more frustrated, he makes shocking statements: "in spite of your manifold attractions, it is by no means certain that another offer of marriage may ever be made to you" (83). He continues to believe that Elizabeth is merely trying to be charming, and the chapter ends with Elizabeth leaving the room, with Collins insisting that she will be brought around as soon as he officially approaches her parents.

Mrs. Bennet returns in **chapter 20** to congratulate Mr. Collins; she is shocked to hear that Elizabeth declined, but Mr. Collins assures her that it was mere modesty and charm. Mrs. Bennet is alarmed nonetheless, and goes to Mr. Bennet to insist that Lizzy marry Collins. Elizabeth is summoned, and Mr. Bennet explains the situation: "An unhappy alternative is before you, Elizabeth. From this day you must be a stranger to one of your parents. Your mother will never see you again if you do not marry Mr. Collins, and I will never see you again if you do" (85). This kind of humor is typical of Mr. Bennet, as are his wife's and daughter's reactions to his comment. Mrs. Bennet is outraged, and Elizabeth is comforted by having her father's immediate understanding of her loathing of Mr. Collins. Mr. Collins is not really upset by the rejection, since ultimately, "His regard for her was quite imaginary" (86). Mrs. Bennet remains dismal and sickly due to Elizabeth's refusal, but the rest of the family agrees that Elizabeth has made the right decision.

In **chapter 21**, Mr. Collins responds to Elizabeth's rejection with "stiffness of manner and resentful silence" (88). The girls walk to Meryton to inquire after Mr. Wickham; he walks back with Elizabeth, and explains his absence from the ball. Elizabeth is pleased by his attentions. Jane receives a letter from Caroline Bingley that surprises and disappoints her; the Bingleys have all left Netherfield for town, and do not intend to return to Hertfordshire any time soon. Even more distressing is Caroline's cruel implication that they are going to visit Mr. Darcy's sister, Georgiana, and that they hope that their brother will marry her. Elizabeth tries to comfort her sister, but is quite incensed at Miss Bingley's behavior. They agree to tell their mother that the party has left Netherfield, but no more; nonetheless, Mrs. Bennet is distressed by the news, although she concludes that he will return soon for a promised dinner in Longbourn.

Elizabeth thanks her friend Charlotte for entertaining Mr. Collins during the day in **Chapter 22**; Charlotte claims it is no sacrifice, and indeed, we soon learn that she hopes to engage Mr. Collins' affections for herself. She succeeds immediately. Mr. Collins proposes, and Sir William and Lady Lucas immediately agree to the match. Charlotte's thoughts on the matter are expressed by the narrator: "Mr. Collins, to be sure, was neither sensible nor agreeable; his society was irksome, and his attachment to her must be imaginary. But still he would be her husband. Without thinking highly either of men or of matrimony, marriage had always been her object; it was the only honorable provision for well-educated young women of small fortune, and however uncertain of giving happiness, must be their pleasantest preservative from want" (94). Charlotte worries that the news may cause a shock to her friend Elizabeth, so she asks Mr. Collins not to tell the Bennets until she first tells Elizabeth. Mr. Collins complies and returns to the Bennets for his last night in their home. The next morning, Charlotte visits Elizabeth and informs her of her engagement, explaining "I am not romantic, you know; I never was. I ask only a comfortable home; and considering Mr. Collins's character, connections, and situation in life, I am convinced that my chance of happiness with him is as fair as most people can boast on entering the marriage state" (96). Elizabeth believes the match completely unsuitable, and worries for her friend, who she believes cannot possibly be happy with her choice.

Before Elizabeth has a chance to tell the family about Charlotte's engagement, Sir William Lucas arrives at the opening of **chapter 23** to announce it himself. They are all greatly shocked by the revelation; Mrs. Bennet is particularly angry at Elizabeth, especially as Mrs. Lucas visits more often, referring to the joys of having a daughter well married. The friendship between Elizabeth and Charlotte grows distant. Elizabeth turns to Jane, who is waiting for a reply to her letter to Caroline Bingley. A laughable letter of thanks arrives from Mr. Collins; unfortunately, it also brings tidings of his plan to visit them again soon. He returns, much to the annoyance of all. Thankfully, he spends most of his time at Lucas Lodge. Mrs. Bennet frets further over the situation of the entail, which means that after Mr. Bennet's death, their home will go to Mr. Collins and Charlotte, a situation that she finds enormously unjust, particularly since they already have a home through the parsonage at Hunsford. This is the end of Volume I of the novel.

Caroline Bingley's letter finally arrives at the beginning of **Volume II, chapter 1**, but it brings no pleasure to Jane. Caroline praises Georgiana Darcy excessively, and continues to imply that she is to be their new sister-in-law. Elizabeth tries to comfort Jane, but the two have different temperaments. Elizabeth claims that Jane "wish[es] to think all the world respectable, and are hurt if I speak ill of any body" (104). Meanwhile, Elizabeth claims "The more I see of the world, the more I am dissatisfied with it; and every day confirms my belief of the inconsistency of all human characters, and of the little dependence that can be placed on the appearance of either merit or sense" (104). Mrs. Bennet continues to speak of Bingley, providing fresh pains for Jane. Their only comfort during this time is Mr. Wickham, who has spread his tale of injustice at the hands of Darcy. Everyone is glad to think well of Wickham and ill of Darcy, so the story is believed immediately.

After a week in Longbourn, Mr. Collins returns to his parish at the opening of **chapter 2**. After his departure, Mr. and Mrs. Gardiner (Mrs. Bennet's brother and his wife) arrive for a visit. The Gardiners are well-bred, sensible, and caring, and Elizabeth and Jane are quite fond of them. After hearing of the attachment between Jane and Mr. Bingley, Mrs. Gardiner suggests that Jane come to London with them for a change of scenery. Mr. Wickham visits, and Mrs. Gardiner observes his preference for Elizabeth (and hers for him). Mrs. Gardiner is familiar with the Pemberley estate (where Wickham grew up with Darcy); she is pleased to share in conversation with Wickham, who is a charming conversationalist. Hearing Wickham's story of Darcy's behavior, she cannot remember anything in particular of Darcy, and chooses to accept Wickham's tale.

In **chapter 3**, Mrs. Gardiner tells Elizabeth that she should not become too attached to Wickham, since neither of them have any means of support. Elizabeth sees the sense in this and promises to try not to become too attached to him. Mr. Collins returns once again, this time for his wedding. Charlotte asks Elizabeth to visit her at her new home in Hunsford, and she promises to do so. Elizabeth receives a letter from Jane in London. Jane is disappointed because Caroline has ignored her while she has been in London, and she has only made one very short, rude visit. Elizabeth is saddened by Jane's disappointment and the rude behavior of Miss Bingley, but she is pleased to be able to write Bingley off finally and completely. Elizabeth writes to Mrs. Gardiner to tell her not to worry about her promise, as Mr. Wickham is no longer showing any interest in her. Indeed, Mr. Wickham has recently been paying his attentions to a Miss King, recent heiress of 10,000 pounds. Elizabeth remains cordial to him, and realizes that her ease in seeing his feelings change indicates that her own feelings for him were not very strong.

Elizabeth passes some dull winter months at home before eagerly making the trip to visit Charlotte at Hunsford with Sir William and his second daughter, Maria in **chapter 4**. She has a friendly farewell with Mr. Wickham. The travelers stop for a night in London, where Elizabeth is able to see Jane and the Gardiners. Mrs. Gardiner is disappointed by the behavior of Wickham, and becomes critical of Miss King (the heiress and new object of Wickham's attentions). The Gardiners propose that Elizabeth join them later in a summer tour of the Lakes, a plan that thrills Elizabeth.

Elizabeth begins the next day, **chapter 5**, in a wonderful mood as she sets out for Hunsford with Sir William and Maria. Upon their arrival, they are welcomed by Mr. Collins with his typical absurd formality. Elizabeth watches Charlotte's reactions to her husband's behavior, and finds that she seems to endure it by ignoring it. It is also clear that Charlotte takes great pride and pleasure in her home. She notes that "When Mr. Collins could be forgotten, there was really a great air of comfort throughout, and by Charlotte's evident enjoyment of it, Elizabeth supposed he must be often forgotten" (121). Mr. Collins goes on about the pleasures and privileges of Lady Catherine de Bourgh, their neighbor and his patron. His excessive praise is interrupted by the arrival of the young Miss de Bourgh and her lady maid, Mrs. Jenkinson. Elizabeth observes to herself that Miss de Bourgh looks "sickly and cross" (122) and is pleased to imagine her as a "proper" wife for Mr. Darcy. Mr. Collins is endlessly delighted to announce that they have been honored by an invitation to dinner at Rosings (the home of the de Bourghs) the following day.

Mr. Collins spends the opening of **chapter 6** preparing his guests for the grandeur of Rosings. Maria and Sir William are nervous about meeting Lady Catherine, but Elizabeth is unconcerned with the pedigree, wealth, and position of Lady de Bourgh. Upon arriving, Elizabeth carefully observes the women of the house. She finds that Mr. Wickham's report of Lady Catherine exactly matches her own observations. She notes that Miss de Bourgh is extremely thin and small, and is constantly attended by Mrs. Jenkinson. Elizabeth watches Mr. Collins and Sir William praise everything about the dinner excessively, and also sees how Lady Catherine enjoys their obsequiousness. Maria and Elizabeth hardly speak at all, while Lady Catherine was constantly "delivering her opinion on every subject in so decisive a manner as proved that she was not used to have her judgment controverted" (126). After dinner, Lady Catherine begins to question Elizabeth rather impertinently about her family's financial situation. She is shocked to learn that the girls had no governess. For the rest of the evening they play cards. Elizabeth returns and gives Charlotte a pleasant review of the evening, simply to be polite.

In **chapter 7**, Sir William leaves Hunsford after a week, but Elizabeth stays on to visit with her friend. They spend the time pleasantly; Elizabeth enjoys the quiet time alone with Charlotte, and endures twice weekly dining at Rosings. After a fortnight, Elizabeth learns that Mr. Darcy will join the party at Rosings, and she looks forward to his arrival merely so that she can observe his behavior and interaction with Lady Catherine and her daughter. Mr. Darcy and Colonel Fitzwilliam call on the Collinses on their second day in the area, a civility that Charlotte immediately attributes to the presence of Elizabeth. Mr. Darcy inquires after Elizabeth's family, and she asks him if he has seen Jane while in London. Although she knows that he hasn't, she hopes he will reveal how much he knows about Miss Bingley's treatment of Jane. Darcy looks confused and answers that he has not seen her; the matter is dropped immediately.

About a week after Mr. Darcy and Colonel Fitzwilliam's arrival, the Collinses and their guests are invited to Rosings on Easter at the beginning of **chapter 8**. Colonel Fitzwilliam finds Elizabeth very pretty, and talks with her with great animation; Elizabeth finds herself enjoying time at Rosings as she never has before. Their lively conversation attracts the attention of Lady Catherine and Mr. Darcy. Lady Catherine interrupts their conversation, dispensing useless advice to the company, and Mr. Darcy seems to be ashamed of his aunt's behavior. Elizabeth plays the piano at Colonel Fitzwilliam's request; Lady Catherine is annoyed to find that Darcy walks away from her in order to listen to Elizabeth's performance. Elizabeth and Darcy begin to tease one another about their own behavior (hers at the piano, his at the dance in Hertfordshire). They seem to enjoy their exchange immensely, but they draw the attention of Lady Catherine, who begins a critique of Elizabeth's playing. Elizabeth observes Darcy's cold reaction to this, as well as his obvious lack of interest in Miss de Bourgh.

Chapter 9 opens with Elizabeth receiving a surprise visit from Mr. Darcy. He and Elizabeth begin a conversation, and Elizabeth expresses her surprise at their hasty departure from Netherfield during the previous fall. Elizabeth drops the subject, and Darcy resumes with a discussion of Charlotte's good fortune in finding a husband and home so near to that of her parents. Elizabeth believes that Hunsford is actually quite far from their home, and the two share their differing views on the advantages of remaining close to home (particularly to Longbourn). When Charlotte and Maria return from their walk, they are shocked to find Mr. Darcy there; he leaves after only a few minutes, prompting Charlotte to exclaim that "he must be in love with you or he would never have called on us in this familiar way" (138). Elizabeth denies this possibility, but Mr. Darcy continues to visit them frequently, and Elizabeth cannot quite determine why.

In **chapter 10**, we learn that Elizabeth has frequently met Mr. Darcy while on her walks in the Park, despite the fact that she has told him where she usually walks in order to deter him from walking the same path as her. One day, joining her on her walk, Mr. Darcy seems to imply that in the future, when she visits Kent, she will stay at Rosings, and Elizabeth wonders if he is alluding to her partiality for Colonel Fitzwilliam. Soon after, Colonel Fitzwilliam meets her on a walk, and speaks to her of his need to consider money when he chooses a wife, since he is a younger son. Colonel Fitzwilliam tells Elizabeth that Darcy recently saved one of his friends from an imprudent marriage, and of course, Elizabeth believes he refers to

Bingley's relationship with Jane. Colonel Fitzwilliam also tells her that he shares with Mr. Darcy the guardianship of Miss Darcy. When Elizabeth jokingly wonders aloud if the girl can need two such guardians, Colonel Fitzwilliam's reaction belies that she has perhaps hit on the truth, but Elizabeth immediately tells him that she has heard nothing but positive stories of Miss Darcy. Later, Elizabeth reflects on the conversation, and becomes convinced that Darcy meddled in Jane and Bingley's relationship. Her anger and worries give her a headache, and she declines to visit Rosings that night, despite Mr. Collins' rebuke that Lady Catherine will be gravely disappointed.

Chapter 11 opens with Elizabeth perusing her letters from Jane while the Collinses are at Rosings. She is surprised by the arrival of Mr. Darcy, who behaves quite strangely, and then declares his love for her in most unusual terms: "In vain have I struggled. It will not do. My feelings will not be repressed. You must allow me to tell you how ardently I admire and love you" (145). This unexpected proclamation is followed by Darcy's catalogue of the various ways in which Elizabeth is an unsuitable match for him, mostly due to her family connections. Surprised by this unexpected confession, and outraged by his insults to her family, Elizabeth sharply refuses him, citing his insults to her, his meddling in the relationship of Bingley and Jane, and his treatment of Wickham as reasons for her distaste for him. Darcy is angry and contemptuous. Elizabeth replies "You could not have made me the offer of your hand in any possible way that would have tempted me to accept it" (148). In particular, Elizabeth cites "his abominable pride" (149) as his most serious flaw. Darcy is astonished, and hastily departs soon after. Elizabeth is left shaken and confused by the events, and she hurries away to her room before Charlotte returns from Rosings.

At the beginning of **chapter 12**, Elizabeth awakes still full of wonder at the encounter with Darcy. She decides to take a walk, specifically in the opposite direction of where she might expect to be intercepted by Darcy. Despite her attempts to avoid him, he finds her, calls her name, and gives her a letter.

He hastily departs, and Elizabeth opens the letter to read it. The letter is reproduced for the reader, and contains Darcy's side of the story. He establishes immediately that he does not intend to further press his suit, but that he wishes to correct two of her accusations from the previous night. First he addresses the issue of why he persuaded Bingley not to marry Jane, citing his opinion of the Bennet family, and the fact that he did not believe that Jane was very much attached to Bingley. He admits to having known that Jane was in London, and that he feels uneasy that he kept this information from Bingley. The second accusation, about his behavior toward Wickham, is a source of great outrage to Darcy. Darcy explains the entirety of Wickham's tale; he was indeed a favorite of Darcy's father, and asked Darcy to promote him professionally as a clergyman. When Wickham declined to become a clergyman, Darcy agreed to give him money (3,000 pounds) to study law; but Wickham abandoned law school quickly and wasted the money. When Wickham returned to Darcy to ask for more money, Darcy refused him. Soon after, Wickham managed to gain the affections of Darcy's younger sister, Georgiana, through a connection he established with Georgiana's governess, Miss Younge. Wickham talked Georgiana into eloping with him. Darcy was able to prevent this outrage, and Georgiana realized the true character of Wickham, who was only after Georgiana's fortune of thirty thousand pounds (and possibly revenge upon Darcy). Darcy explains that Elizabeth can ask Colonel Fitzwilliam to verify all of the information he has given her, and he closes with "God bless you" (156); the chapter ends with the end of Darcy's letter. At this point in the novel, we have witnessed the exchange of many letters among various characters. During Austen's time, letter writing was of course quite popular, as it was the only means of communicating over long distances. There were many formal rules of etiquette regarding correspondence between unmarried men and women in particular. Had Darcy sent his letter to Elizabeth via the post, it would have indicated to others that the two were engaged. His hand delivery of the letter to Elizabeth is explained by his following this custom. This also serves to explain why Elizabeth does not write a response to him, as well as why Jane and Bingley, despite their mutual friendship, did not correspond in between their meetings. It is important to note that the novel itself was originally conceived as an epistolary novel, meaning a novel written as a series of letters. **Chapter 13** concerns Elizabeth's response to the shocking letter. She initially read the letter "with a strong prejudice against everything he might say" (156). She refuses to believe his claims at first, and "Astonishment, apprehension, and even horror, oppressed her" (156). She rereads every sentence closely, and begins to rethink her acquaintance with Wickham. She realizes that his behavior was suspect all along, and his attentions to Miss King, seen in the light of his behavior towards Georgiana, makes his mercenary designs clear. She begins to realize her grave misjudgments of both Wickham and Darcy, and is deeply ashamed of herself. She still is not satisfied by Darcy's recounting of the relationship between Jane and Bingley, but on a second reading of the letter, she realizes that Jane's behavior was not that of a woman in love, and that Darcy might easily have missed the signs of Jane's deep affection for Bingley. She is pained by Darcy's comments on her family's behavior, but finds his critiques just, and feels some little pleasure at the complement that he offers to both Jane and Elizabeth, who rise far above their parents and sisters in his estimation. She eventually returns home, and is told that Darcy and Colonel Fitzwilliam called while she was away. She is glad that she missed them, and can think only of the letter.

In **chapter 14**, Darcy and Fitzwilliam depart Rosings, and Mr. Collins goes to "console" Lady Catherine. He is pleased to then receive an invitation for the whole family to go to Rosings that night. Elizabeth realizes that had she behaved differently the night before, she might be attending Rosings as Lady Catherine's future niece, and she is pleased to imagine Lady Catherine's indignation at this possibility. Lady Catherine insists that Elizabeth should stay another fortnight at least, but she explains that she must return home; Lady Catherine proceeds to give extensive advice on the manner of their trip home. Elizabeth spends the next few days rereading the letter and reflecting on her actions. She does not regret her refusal of Darcy's proposal, but does realize that she has behaved unjustly towards him. She is saddened by the thought of her silly sisters and mother, and fears that there is nothing to be done to improve their behavior, which she sees now has cost Jane her happiness with Bingley.

Chapter 15 opens with Mr. Collins' excessive civilities over breakfast on their last day in Hunsford. Elizabeth and Maria depart eagerly, though Elizabeth is sad to leave her friend Charlotte. They stop at the Gardiner's house on the way, and Elizabeth has the pleasure of seeing Jane, who will join them on the rest of the journey home. She wonders how much of the letter she should share with Jane, and how the news of Bingley's behavior will affect her sister.

Elizabeth and Jane arrive at an inn along the way home in **chapter 16** and are immediately greeted by their sisters Kitty and Lydia. They have prepared an elaborate lunch to treat their elder sisters, but reveal that they have spent all their money at the local shops, so Elizabeth and Jane must cover the bill. Elizabeth is thankful that the militia will soon leave Meryton, news that has profoundly upset Kitty and Lydia. Kitty and Lydia share other gossip, including the fact that Miss King has departed, and Wickham is once again available. On the drive home, Lydia asks whether her sisters have met any men or done any flirting while away, and rudely comments about Jane becoming an old maid. Their reception at home is as expected, with Mr. Bennet pleased to have Lizzy back and Mrs. Bennet fawning over Jane. That night the Lucases arrive to meet Maria and hear about their trip. That afternoon, Lydia urges the others to walk with her to Meryton; Elizabeth declines so as to avoid seeing Wickham. Lydia has talked of going to Brighton, where the militia will be stationed next. Elizabeth is relieved that her father has no intention of letting her go, but still wonders at her mother's eagerness to allow Lydia to visit the regiment so often.

In **chapter 17**, Elizabeth decides to tell Jane about the strange events with Darcy, but she will not tell Jane anything about the situation with Bingley, fearing to cause her pain. Jane is surprised to learn of Darcy's proposal, particularly his offensive means of making it, but she believes her sister completely worthy of Darcy. She does not blame her for refusing Darcy, but is saddened by the thought of how hurt Darcy must have been by the refusal. Elizabeth then goes on to tell her all about Wickham's wickedness, which shocks and grieves Jane, who wishes to think well of everyone. Together they decide not to tell anyone about Wickham's true character, since it would be very difficult to do without telling the story about his treatment of Miss Darcy, which they do not wish to become public. Elizabeth is still troubled by the question of whether or not to tell Jane about Darcy's role in breaking off her relationship with Bingley, but for now she decides not to share the information. Mrs. Bennet tells Elizabeth how deeply disappointed she is by Jane's loss of Mr. Bingley, mostly because of his great wealth. She goes on to complain about the injustice of the Collinses receiving Longbourn due to the entail.

Kitty and Lydia are disappointed at the impending departure of the militia at the beginning of **chapter 18**, but Mrs. Forster, the wife of the colonel of the regiment, invites Lydia to travel with her to Brighton, and she is ecstatic. Mr. Bennet caves in to her demands, saying "We shall have no peace at Longbourne if Lydia does not go to Brighton" (177). He actually believes that the trip will have a good effect on her, since her lack of money and connections will not make her the object of any mercenary, and "she will be of less importance even as a common flirt than she has been here" (177). Elizabeth sees Wickham frequently at various dinners during this chapter, and on the night before the regiment departs, they have an encounter that leaves Wickham uneasy. Elizabeth does not tell Wickham what she knows, but she mentions that while she was at Hunsford, she spent nearly every day of three weeks in the company of Colonel Fitzwilliam and Mr. Darcy. He seems unnerved by this, and tries to get more information, but Elizabeth makes herself cordially unavailable. Lydia leaves for Meryton with Mrs. Forster that night, and they plan to go to Brighton in the morning.

In **chapter 19**, we learn a bit of the background story of Mr. and Mrs. Bennet. Mr. Bennet married his wife because of her youth and beauty, and very early in their marriage lost any real regard or affection for her. He amuses himself with her silliness and with his own pleasures of reading and living in the country. Elizabeth is pained to see this, and especially to observe how careless Mr. Bennet has been in the raising of his daughters. After the loss of the militia, Mrs. Bennet and Kitty become unbearable to Elizabeth, as there are many fewer social events to placate and entertain them. Elizabeth's hope is that Kitty will improve herself in the absence of the flighty and uncontrolled influence of Lydia. Elizabeth's only real pleasure is the anticipation of touring the lakes with the Gardiners. The Gardiners eventually arrive at Longbourn, stay for one night; they leave their four children in the care of Jane and take Elizabeth with them on their tour, which will pass near Pemberley, the home of Mr. Darcy. Mrs. Gardiner is eager to visit, but Elizabeth is just as eager to avoid it, fearful of meeting Mr. Darcy. Later that night, she questions the inn's chambermaid and is relieved to learn that Mr. Darcy is not currently at home. The next morning she indicates, with feigned indifference, that she is willing to visit Pemberley. This is the end of the second volume.

Volume III, chapter 1 details the many splendors of Pemberley in considerable detail. Elizabeth finds it delightful, and she thinks "that to be mistress of Pemberley might be something!" (185). While she briefly thinks of how wonderful it might be to live at Pemberley, she is brought back to reality by the belief that if she were, she would lose her beloved family (particularly her aunt and uncle who have brought her here) and pushes further longing from her mind. The housekeeper, Mrs. Reynolds, gives a tour of areas of the home, explaining the histories of people in the various portraits. She explains that Mr. Wickham "has turned out very wild" (186) and that Mr. Darcy was an exceedingly good-natured child and is now a much-beloved master. Elizabeth also learns that Miss Darcy is an accomplished musician and very attractive. Elizabeth is particularly moved by Mr. Darcy's kindness and generosity to his sister, and it becomes clear that she has misjudged a kind and noble man. She thinks "What praise is more valuable than the praise of an intelligent servant?" (189). Not many servants are actually seen in this novel, although they undoubtedly fill the corners of the story (chambermaids, innkeepers, cooks, gardeners and all manner of other servants). Austen's comment here accords a level of elevation to the opinion of the servant, but excepting her ability to comment on Darcy, she is not an important figure to the narrative. Elizabeth only wants to hear more of Mr. Darcy, and the next moment, the man himself appears most unexpectedly. There is no way to avoid him. Both Elizabeth and Darcy are clearly surprised and somewhat awkward in their meeting, but Elizabeth is impressed and a little unnerved by Darcy's perfect civility. He immediately asks about her family, which again seems surprising given his harsh description of them during his proposal and in his letter. When he takes his leave of her, she is mortified, and wonders what he must think of her. She is surprised once again when Darcy returns more appropriately dressed and asks her to introduce him to her aunt and uncle. Elizabeth believes that he will immediately depart when he realizes their social status, but he once again surprises her by engaging in extended conversation with Mr. Gardiner. Listening to their conversation, Elizabeth is pleased that Darcy has met one member of her family of whom she need not be embarrassed; Mr. Gardiner is smart, well-mannered, and tasteful. Darcy invites Mr. Gardiner to fish at Pemberley whenever he wishes, and they are overwhelmed and impressed by his regard and generosity. Elizabeth and Darcy walk together for a while, and Elizabeth informs him that she had believed that Darcy would not be at Pemberley, or else she would not have visited. He explains that he came home early in order to prepare for his sister, and then asks if Elizabeth will join their party (which will include Bingley and his sisters) in order to meet Miss Darcy. Once again surprised by these attentions from Darcy, Elizabeth accepts the invitation. When they leave, the Gardiners discuss the pleasures of Darcy's civility, as they have also heard tales of his disagreeable nature and abominable treatment of Wickham. Elizabeth indicates that Wickham's story may not have been true.

At the opening of **chapter 2**, Elizabeth is surprised by a visit from Darcy and his sister on the very day of her arrival. When Elizabeth explains to the Gardiners who their visitor is, the Gardiners immediately begin to suspect that Darcy is partial to their niece, as there is no other explanation for such attention. Both Elizabeth and Miss Darcy seem embarrassed by their meeting, and Elizabeth immediately sees that Miss Darcy is very shy (not, as Wickham claimed, exceedingly proud). Bingley arrives soon after, and makes civil inquiries about her family. Elizabeth thinks sadly of Jane, and observes that Miss Darcy and Bingley do not seem to entertain any personal affection for one another. Bingley mentions to her the exact date of his last dance with Jane, with a note of sadness in his voice, and Elizabeth is pleased that he still seems to remember Jane fondly. Bingley and the Darcys depart after inviting the Gardiners and Elizabeth to dinner at Pemberley. The Gardiners are absolutely convinced that Mr. Darcy is very much in love with Elizabeth, though they feel no need to question her about it. They also begin to hear negative reports of Wickham from others in the area, and they believe most assuredly that Mr. Darcy is a wholly agreeable and honorable man. Mrs. Gardiner and Elizabeth agree to visit Miss Darcy the next morning, since she was so kind and polite as to visit them on her first day at Pemberley.

At the beginning of **chapter 3**, Elizabeth realizes that since Miss Bingley's dislike of her was the result of jealousy, she will not be particularly welcome by her at Pemberley. The thought does not seriously worry her, however, and she is merely more interested in observing how she will behave. Elizabeth and Mrs. Gardiner arrive at the house and Miss Darcy is very civil, although still quite shy. Bingley's sisters have very little to say, and the conversation is filled with awkward pauses. Most of the conversation is carried by another guest, Mrs. Annesley, Mrs. Gardiner, and Elizabeth, who realizes that Miss Bingley is watching her very closely. She both wishes and fears that Mr. Darcy will join them. When he does, Miss Bingley joins the conversation, pointedly asking Elizabeth how the militia's departure from Meryton has affected her family. Her snide comment immediately brings Wickham to mind for all in the room, however, Miss Bingley does not know how disturbing her implication is. The Bingleys know nothing of Georgiana's elopement, as Darcy has kept the information in greatest secrecy. Elizabeth is able to maintain her composure and prevent any revelation. Miss Darcy is clearly upset by the reference, but Miss Bingley remains unaware of the cause. Darcy only becomes more interested in Elizabeth, the exact opposite effect that Miss Bingley had intended. After Mrs. Gardiner and Elizabeth depart, Miss Bingley harshly criticizes Elizabeth's appearance. Georgiana refuses to join in, and Mr. Darcy coolly repels the comments. Miss Bingley reminds him that he once agreed with her that Elizabeth was not attractive, but Mr. Darcy responds that he now believes her "one of the handsomest women of my acquaintance" (205) and leaves the room. Elizabeth and Mrs. Gardiner discuss their experiences of the day, but both shy away from a direct discussion of Darcy, despite the fact that they both wish to discuss him exclusively.

Elizabeth finally receives two long-awaited letters from Jane in **chapter 4**. The first letter begins normally, but the second half indicates the extreme agitation of the writer. Jane informs her that Colonel Forster sent an express letter to tell the family that Lydia had run off with Wickham to Scotland, where minors can marry without parental permission. Kitty seems unsurprised by the information. Elizabeth turns to the second letter, which contains still more bad news. Although the idea of a marriage between Wickham and Lydia seemed like a bad idea, the family now worries that they have not even married; such a thing would be beyond scandalous for the time. Other militia men indicate that Wickham never intended to marry Lydia at all. Jane continues to believe that they must have married, but Mr. and Mrs. Bennet believe the worst. Jane begs Elizabeth to return home, and to enlist the aid of Mr. Gardiner. Their father intends to go to London to find Wickham and Lydia, but Jane thinks that it would be better if Mr. Gardiner went with him. Finishing the letter, Elizabeth rapidly seeks her aunt and uncle, but instead finds Mr. Darcy. He offers to send a servant to gather the Gardiners, and ask Elizabeth if he can be of assistance. She explains the situation to him; he is shocked and offers the few words of consolation and concern he can. Elizabeth realizes that such dishonorable behavior in her family will finally and forever part her from a possible future with Darcy, and at this moment, "never had she so honestly felt that she could have loved him, as now, when all love must be in vain" (210). She believes she may never see him again as they have upon this visit, and she is doubly pained by the upsetting events at home for their desperate consequences for herself. Elizabeth is convinced that Wickham had no intention of marrying Lydia, particularly since she has no money to recommend her. She also realizes that Lydia was easy prey for Wickham, and profoundly regrets her parents' indulgence of such a silly and unrestrained girl. The Gardiners hear the news with great alarm, and they immediately prepare for a journey to Longbourn. Mrs. Gardiner has learned from a servant that Darcy was present, and Elizabeth informs her that he knows what has happened. Mrs. Gardiner again wonders at the intimacy between the two, but says nothing to Elizabeth.

Chapter 5 begins on the road to Longbourn, where Mr. Gardiner tries to encourage Elizabeth with hopes that Wickham must intend to marry Lydia. Elizabeth knows too much of Wickham's history and character to be at all comforted by this, and instead she blames herself for not having revealed what she knew. They arrive at Longbourn the next day; Jane and Elizabeth meet with great affection on both sides. Jane informs her that their father has been in London for a few days, but has written only once, and with no news of Wickham or Lydia. Their mother has remained in her dressing room, which is a blessing, since it will keep the servants from knowing the details of the affair. Mrs. Bennet blames the Forsters for neglect, and insists that if she herself had been allowed to take Lydia to Brighton, as she had begged Mr. Bennet, that none of this would have happened. She is fearful that Mr. Bennet may kill Wickham when he finds him, resulting in the family being turned out of Longbourn by the Collinses. Mr. Gardiner comforts his sister by telling her that he will follow Mr. Bennet to London and prevent this from happening. Kitty and Mary seem unconcerned about the scandal. Mary makes the situation into a lesson in morality: "that loss of virtue in female is irretrievable—that one false step involves her in endless ruin—that her reputation is no less brittle than it is beautiful" (219). While these sentiments are indeed true in this society, their statement at this moment, by a sister seems particularly harsh and cold-hearted. Jane shares with Elizabeth all the details she has of Lydia's elopement, and together they read over the letter that Lydia left for Harriet Forster. It is a careless and silly letter, including a request for a servant to mend one of her dresses before they send her things on to Longbourn. Despite Lydia's giddy tone, the letter does clearly indicate that she expects to marry Wickham, which at least gives them the comfort of knowing that she had not planned such a dishonor, and was no doubt being played by Wickham. Elizabeth is concerned about how many servants are acquainted with the particulars of the situation. Jane tells her that some of their friends—Aunt Phillips and the Lucases—have visited to offer comfort and assistance. Elizabeth responds that "under such a misfortune as this, one cannot see too little of one's neighbors. Assistance is impossible; condolence, insufferable. Let them triumph at a distance, and be satisfied" (222).

Mr. Gardiner leaves for London at the opening of **chapter 6**, and Mrs. Gardiner remains at Longbourn to assist the family there. Throughout Meryton, word spreads of Wickham's despicable behavior. He has debts with every tradesman in town and is declared "the wickedest young man in the world" (223). These stories make Elizabeth more certain of her sister's ruin. Longbourn is full of anxiety, and the post is awaited each day with great impatience. Mr. Gardiner writes to explain his plans to find Wickham using information from his fellows in the regiment. Another letter arrives from Mr. Collins offering condolences; he claims that "the death of your daughter would have been a blessing in comparison of this" (225). He criticizes the Bennets for their lack of discipline, and reports on Lady Catherine's response to the whole affair, saying that no one will want to marry any of the girls for fear of joining into such a scandalous family. His final advice is that Mr. Bennet should "throw off your unworthy child from your affection for ever, and leave her to reap the fruits of her own heinous offence" (225). Another letter arrives from Mr. Gardiner, but it offers no information on the whereabouts of Lydia and Wickham, although he has learned that Wickham has accumulated over a thousand pounds in gambling debts, in addition to large tabs at local merchants. Disheartened by the failure of the search, Mr. Bennet returns to Longbourn and Mrs. Gardiner departs Longbourn for her own home. Mr. Bennet is very quiet upon his return; he realizes his own culpability in the behavior of his daughter, and tells Elizabeth that he should have heeded her advice about refusing to allow Lydia to go to Brighton. He claims that he intends to be much more strict with Kitty, much to Kitty's displeasure.

In **chapter 7**, Mr. Bennet finally receives word from Mr. Gardiner explaining the situation in London. He shares the letter with Jane and Elizabeth, who read it aloud. Lydia and Wickham have been found. For them to be married, Mr. Bennet must agree to provide her with an income of one hundred pounds per year, plus an equal share of the inheritance after his death. Mr. Gardiner has acted on his behalf in this negotiation, and now only desires Mr. Bennets approval. Mr. Gardiner claims that Wickham's debts are not nearly so much as others have claimed, and that Lydia will be married immediately at the Gardiners' home. Mr. Bennet assumes that Mr. Gardiner has paid Wickham a large sum of money (he suggests that it might be as much as ten thousand pounds), which he will need to repay, but he hastily responds to the letter with his acceptance. Jane and Elizabeth share the letter with their mother and others sisters; Mrs. Bennet is delighted and begins to concern herself with wedding clothes. Elizabeth is grateful for the marriage, but disturbed that it should come about in such away, and ashamed of her mother's silly behavior.

Mr. Bennet worries considerably about how much money Mr. Gardiner has paid to arrange Lydia and Wickham's marriage. At the beginning of **chapter 8**, he informs Mrs. Bennet that he will not receive them at Longbourn, nor will he provide any money for wedding clothing. Mrs. Bennet is horrified, and more concerned about the lack of proper wedding clothes and parties than she is about the scandalous behavior of her daughter in eloping. Elizabeth thinks of Darcy, and realizes that with Wickham as her brother-in-law, Darcy could not possibly consider joining with her family. She is despondent, and realizes "he was exactly the man, who, in disposition and talents, would most suit her" (237). Mr. Bennet receives another letter from Mr. Gardiner with further details on Wickham's plans. He will pay off all of his debts in Brighton and Meryton, and leave the militia for a new position currently located in the North of England. Jane, Elizabeth, and Mr. Bennet all see the wisdom in their living far from Longbourn, since the scandal is still so freshly attached to them. But Mrs. Bennet is greatly displeased by the news. Jane and Elizabeth convince Mr. Bennet to receive the couple at Longbourn before their travels North. Elizabeth feels that seeing Wickham is the last thing she could possibly wish for, but is relieved that Lydia will be accepted back into the family after her behavior.

Chapter 9 brings the arrival of Mr. and Mrs. Wickham. Mrs. Bennet is joyful, Mr. Bennet is grave, and the girls are all anxious and serious. Lydia and Wickham are unconcerned with the trouble they have caused, and show no sense of shame in their actions. Lydia demands congratulations from her sisters and is her usual exuberant, careless self. Wickham's manners are still pleasing to everyone. It is clear to Elizabeth that Lydia is very much in love with Wickham, but that he is not terribly interested in her. Lydia goes on about the wedding, and is careless of and ungrateful for everything that the Gardiners have done to save her reputation. She is also rude to her sister, telling Jane that she must move down a seat at the table, since, as a married woman she takes precedence at the table. While such attention to formal details would have been typical during Austen's period, it is rather absurd in this case, as Lydia's means of becoming a married woman are far from traditional. Her behavior is similar to that of her mother, with all attention to silly formalities and a complete ignorance of more grave matters of conduct and propriety. Lydia accidentally lets slip that Darcy attended her wedding, a fact that Elizabeth finds completely unaccountable. Elizabeth writes to Mrs. Gardiner requesting to know why, after Lydia tells her that she was not supposed to mention his presence at all. **Chapter 10** brings Mrs. Gardiner's response to Elizabeth's inquiries regarding Darcy's presence at Lydia's wedding. She informs her that it was Darcy who discovered Wickham, and bribed him with his new job and payment of his various debts. Mr. Darcy then approached Mr. Gardiner with the details, and managed to have him arrange the particulars of the wedding without exposing Darcy's involvement to the Bennets. It seems that Darcy felt that the situation was partly his fault, since he did not expose Wickham's bad character earlier. Mrs. Gardiner reveals how much she likes Darcy, and makes references to the fact that Darcy's actions are the result of his love for Elizabeth; she believes the two would be an excellent match. The letter deeply touches Elizabeth, who realizes how much he has done for her and her whole family. However, she still believes that the shame on her family, and their connection with Wickham will prevent his renewing his proposal to her. Soon after she reads the letter, Wickham opens a conversation with her, during which she guardedly implies that she knows more about his unpleasant history than he might like. She ends the conversation by telling him that they are now brother and sister, and that she hopes they will put the past behind them for good. Her kindness is all for her sister's sake, as she wishes to have the Wickhams out of the house as soon as possible.

Lydia and Wickham depart for Newcastle at the beginning of **chapter 11**. Mrs. Bennet is very sad to see her daughter go, as they probably will not see one another for at least a year. Lydia continues to be self-involved, saying that she probably will not have much time to write to her family since she is now a married woman, but that her sisters, since they are not married, should write often, since they will have little else to do. Mr. Wickham is much more affectionate in his leave-taking than Lydia, and Mr. Bennet is ultimately amused with and pleased by him. Mrs. Bennet's sadness is soon relieved by news from Mrs. Phillips that Mr. Bingley is expected at Netherfield again soon. Elizabeth believes that Bingley is still partial to Jane, and that perhaps Darcy has revealed further information to Bingley, and perhaps approved of the match. She does not speak of any of this to Jane, who tries to be casual, and does not think she will see much of Bingley or his sisters after their recent treatment of her. Mrs. Bennet again insists that Mr. Bennet should visit Mr. Darcy, but he derides her inane attention to etiquette: "You forced me into visiting him last year, and promised if I went to see him, he should marry one of my daughters. But it ended in nothing, and I will not be sent on a fool's errand again" (253). All the talk of Bingley is terribly exhausting and embarrassing to Jane, who wishes no longer to think of Bingley or be reminded of what happened last year. Annoyed as ever with her husband, Mrs. Bennet insists that she will invite Bingley to dinner. But before such an invitation can be dispatched, Bingley arrives with Mr. Darcy. Both Jane and Elizabeth are enormously uncomfortable, but their mother is heedless of their concerns. Mrs. Bennet is obviously cold to Mr. Darcy, particularly in comparison to her warm welcome to Bingley. This is particularly painful to Elizabeth, who knows how much her family owes to Darcy. Elizabeth is mortified when Mrs. Bennet goes on about Lydia's marriage to Wickham, and continues to make officious offers of hospitality to Bingley while nearly insulting Darcy. Elizabeth's one relief from these shameful observations comes from seeing how quickly Bingley warms to Jane and their previous intimacy seems to return within a few minutes. Mrs. Bennet invites the men for dinner, insisting that Bingley owed them this visit since the previous year, when he departed so hastily from Netherfield.

The promised dinner party is the subject of **chapter 12**. Before the gathering, Jane insists that she was not at all disturbed by Bingley's visit, and feels perfectly easy with their civil friendship. Elizabeth tells her that the only danger is that Bingley will fall in love with her again. At the dinner, Elizabeth observes that Bingley is clearly still enamored of Jane. Darcy is unfortunately seated next to Mrs. Bennet and far from Elizabeth, so the two have little chance to talk. After dinner, they do have an opportunity to speak briefly, but Elizabeth cannot do much more than inquire after his sister. After the party, Mrs. Bennet is enormously pleased with herself, and believes she will soon have another daughter married off.

Mr. Bingley calls a few days after the dinner at the opening of **chapter 13**. He informs them that Darcy has gone to London, but will return in ten days. Mrs. Bennet invites him to dinner the following day. Mrs. Bennet does everything in her power to contrive to get Bingley and Jane alone, much to Jane's alarm. Mr. Bingley and Mr. Bennet arrange to hunt the next morning, and it is a pleasurable experience for both of them. Mrs. Bennet contrives again to get Jane and Bingley alone together, and this time she is successful. When Elizabeth returns to the drawing room, the two are in earnest conversation, Bingley whispers something to Jane, and then leaves quickly. Jane is overwhelmed with joy, and tells her sister that she is the happiest woman in the world. After receiving her sister's congratulations, she goes to her mother to tell her the news of her betrothal to Bingley. Mr. Bingley has already gone to speak with Mr. Bennet. Mr. Bingley returns and Elizabeth offers her heartfelt congratulations to her new brother. Mr. Bennet tells Jane that he is very pleased with Bingley and believes that they make a very good match. Jane tells her sister that she was much relieved to learn that Bingley never knew she was in London, which accounted for his not visiting her. However, this makes her wonder at the bad behavior of Miss Bingley; though she hopes they will be pleased to see their brother happy with Jane, she realizes that they will never be as close as they were previously. Soon all of Meryton knows of the engagement, and the Bennets are considered to be a very lucky family. Their recent scandal with Lydia is immediately forgotten in favor of this joyful news.

Chapter 14 opens with a surprise visit from Lady Catherine. Upon her arrival, she is her usual arrogant and ungracious self. Mrs. Bennet is in awe of this woman, and tries to be formal; she asks after Mr. and Mrs. Collins. Elizabeth cannot imagine why she has come here, and believes that perhaps she has a letter for her from Charlotte. Lady Catherine refuses the offers of hospitality from Mrs. Bennet, and rather abruptly requests that Elizabeth join her outside for a walk. Once outside, Lady Catherine informs Elizabeth that she has come because she had heard a rumor that Elizabeth and Darcy are to be married. Elizabeth is shocked, both at the rumor and Lady Catherine's presumption in making such a rude inquiry. Elizabeth refuses to answer directly, and Lady Catherine outright forbids Elizabeth to marry Darcy. She claims that Darcy is engaged to her daughter, claiming that they have been intended to one another since infancy. Elizabeth is unconcerned by Lady Catherine's threats, which infuriates her. Lady Catherine claims that Elizabeth "will be censured, slighted, and despised, by every one connected with him. Your alliance will be a disgrace; your name will never even be mentioned by any of us" (271). Lady Catherine presses her, and Elizabeth reveals that she is not (yet) engaged to Darcy; Lady Catherine demands her to promise that she will not enter into an engagement with him, and Elizabeth outright refuses her, to the considerable outrage of Lady Catherine. Ironically, Lady Catherine's attempt to prevent the impending engagement only serves to make Elizabeth desire it more strongly. Lady Catherine departs greatly incensed and insisting that she will prevent their union.

Chapter 15 opens with Elizabeth's confusion after her encounter with Lady Catherine. She worries that she will influence Darcy not to propose, at the same time that she wonders how and where Lady Catherine heard about the possible engagement in the first place. The next morning, Mr. Bennet talks to Elizabeth about a letter he has received from Mr. Collins. He believes that the two of them will have a good laugh over it, as he tells her that Mr. Collins has heard that Mr. Darcy may propose to Elizabeth, and he advises that she should decline the offer, as Lady Catherine does not wish them to marry. Mr. Bennet believes that Elizabeth will think this a grand joke, since he believes that Darcy would never consider her, and that Elizabeth hates him. Mr. Collins goes on to comment further on the Bennet household, scolding Mr. Bennet for receiving Lydia and Wickham in their home, as "you ought certainly to forgive them as a Christian, but never admit them in your sight, or allow their names to be mentioned in your hearing" (278). Elizabeth manages to hide her mortification from her father, but she is further concerned about what Lady Catherine might be doing behind the scenes to prevent Darcy from proposing.

Mr. Bingley and Mr. Darcy visit a few days later in **chapter 16.** Jane, Bingley, Elizabeth, and Darcy end up on a walk in pairs, and Elizabeth finally has the opportunity to tell Darcy how grateful she and the family are for his intervention in the Wickham affair. Darcy wishes that Mrs. Gardiner had not told her of his involvement, but also indicates that he did it expressly for Elizabeth. There is an awkward silence between them; Darcy confesses that his feelings for her have not changed since his proposal, but if she too is unchanged, he will never speak of it again. Elizabeth hastily and joyfully expresses her change of heart, and the two are delighted to share their mutual affection for one another. They extend their walk far from home. Darcy tells her that Lady Catherine visited him after he came to Longbourn, and told her just how obstinate Elizabeth had been in refusing to reject the notion of marrying Darcy. She had demanded that Darcy promise not to propose, but instead, her story of Elizabeth's behavior only gave Darcy reason to hope that her feelings for him had changed. They both apologize for their behavior during the previous proposal. It was Elizabeth's comment that he had not behaved as a gentleman that had profoundly humbled Darcy, and made him rethink his behavior, and deeply regret his previous excessive pride. Darcy asks if she still has the letter that he gave her the morning after the rejected proposal; she confesses that she does, and agrees that at his request, she will burn it. The two wish to think no more of the letter. The two discuss their surprise meeting at Pemberley, and Darcy explains his serious attempts to prove himself to be a gentleman to her. They suddenly realize that they have not seen Bingley and Jane for some time, and they discuss their engagement. Darcy did in fact talk to Bingley and confess that he had hidden the fact of Jane's presence in London, and had given Bingley his approval for the match. Bingley quickly forgave his friend for his interference, and it is with the intention of renewing his suit with Jane that he returned to Netherfield with Darcy.

Chapter 17 brings the couple back to Longbourn, where Jane wonders at their long absence, but does not suspect anything. Elizabeth knows herself to be happy, but manages to maintain a calm façade; Darcy remains composed as ever. Elizabeth worries about how the family, who have come to find Darcy annoying, will take the news of their engagement. Later that night, she confesses everything to an incredulous Jane, who at first thinks she is joking. Elizabeth must tell her the whole of their history, including what Darcy did for Lydia. Jane is impressed and immensely happy for her sister, though filled with wonder that Elizabeth kept so much from her for so long. The next morning, Mrs. Bennet is annoyed to see Mr. Darcy join Mr. Bingley in a visit to Longbourn. She begs Elizabeth to walk with Darcy to keep him out of the way, and Elizabeth complies quite happily. On their walk, they agree that Darcy will ask Mr. Bennet's approval that evening, and that Elizabeth will tell her mother the news. She wonders how her mother will react, but is sure that it will be excessive, and is glad that she will be able to spare Darcy's witnessing her mother's foolishness. After Mr. Darcy speaks to Mr. Bennet, Mr. Bennet wishes to speak to Elizabeth. He confesses that he finds it hard to believe that Elizabeth will be happy in this marriage, and that despite his money, if Elizabeth hates him (as he believes her to) then she should not marry him. Elizabeth manages to convince him of her love for Darcy, and further explains that Darcy is responsible for clearing up the mess with Wickham and Lydia. Mr. Bennet is shocked but ultimately pleased, for it means that he will not have to repay the money to Mr. Gardiner, as he had previously believed. He laughs at the memory of Mr. Collins' letter of the previous day, and makes a joke about sending in other young men to marry Kitty and Mary. Elizabeth then goes to tell her mother the news. Mrs. Bennet is shocked and silenced for a few moments, but upon recovery, she is instantly thrilled at the thought of how rich this will make Elizabeth. "Jane's is nothing to it" she exclaims (290), thinking only of the comparison of wealth between Bingley and

Darcy. She apologizes for thinking ill of Darcy, and comments on how handsome he is. The next morning, Mrs. Bennet is much more attentive and kind to Darcy, and Mr. Bennet finds that he is a very likeable man.

With most of the major plot twists resolved, **chapter 18** opens with playful dialogue between Elizabeth and Darcy, who discusses how he fell in love with her and the various delays in his making his second proposal. Elizabeth believes that he became interested in her simply because she was not interested in pleasing him, as all the other ladies he met were. He confesses that his proposal was mostly the result of Lady Catherine's misguided intervention, and this reminds the two that they need to share their news with her. Darcy goes to write to Lady Catherine, and Elizabeth writes to Mrs. Gardiner. Mr. Bennet writes to Mr. Collins informing him of the engagement, and advising him to console Lady Catherine, but to stand by Darcy, since "he has more to give" (293). Miss Bingley congratulates her brother and Jane on their engagement, but she is obviously insincere. Nonetheless, Jane writes her a kind response. Miss Darcy, on the other hand, is genuinely delighted by the news of her brother's engagement to Elizabeth. The Collinses soon arrive at Lucas Lodge; it turns out that Lady Catherine was so enraged by the news from Darcy that Charlotte thought it wise to avoid Rosings for a while. Elizabeth is genuinely pleased to see her old friend, although it is painful to watch Mr. Collins' obsequiousness towards Mr. Darcy, in combination with the usual silliness of her own mother and her aunt, Mrs. Phillips. Mrs. Bennet is excessively proud of her daughters' marriages, and Elizabeth cannot wait to leave for Pemberley to escape the constant exhibition of her mother's behavior.

In the final chapter, **chapter 19**, Jane and Elizabeth are married to their respective husbands, much to Mrs. Bennet's pleasure. Mr. Bennet frequently visits Elizabeth and Darcy at Pemberley. Mr. Bingley and Jane leave Netherfield after a year, a move that is attributed to the need to get a farther distance from Mrs. Bennet and other Meryton relatives. Kitty has the pleasure (and improvement) of spending most of her time with her two sisters, while Mary stays home to keep her mother company and entertain her by joining her on visits. Lydia writes to congratulate her sister, and in her letter implies that Wickham would like a promotion in his military appointment and that they could use some more money. Elizabeth responds that she cannot ask Darcy for any help with Wickham, nor any money, but she does end up sending them some money on a regular basis, from the money she saves from her own private expenses. Lydia and Wickham's situation is not ideal; the two spend beyond their means and are constantly moving in order to find a better or cheaper place. "His affection for her soon sunk into indifference; hers lasted a little longer; and in spite of her youth and her manners, she retained all the claims to reputation which her marriage had given her" (296). This passage from the narrator implies that although they do not exactly live happily ever after, they remain married, and Lydia doesn't involve herself in any questionable behavior after the gross misstep of her engagement. Miss Bingley realizes that she must behave better if she wishes to continue being a guest at Pemberley, and she becomes a model of civility. Georgiana and Elizabeth admire one another exceedingly and Darcy is pleased to see them so fond of one another. Georgiana is in awe of Elizabeth's easy way with Darcy, whom she has always treated with the utmost reverence. Lady Catherine's indignation at Darcy and Elizabeth's marriage continued for a while, but Elizabeth encouraged Darcy to reconcile with her, and eventually Lady Catherine paid a visit to Pemberley. The Gardiners make many visits to Pemberley, and Darcy and Elizabeth are very fond of them for their role in bringing the two together. Thus the two most agreeable sisters, Elizabeth and Jane, are settled happily and there is every indication of their future happiness. Lydia and Charlotte are not particularly unhappy, but it is clear that their choices in marriage were not ideal, and they do not enjoy the same degree of pleasure and joy in their marital attachments as the primary couples.

Works Cited

Austen, Jane. *Pride and Prejudice*. Oxford: Oxford University Press, 1998.

Critical Views

E.M. HALLIDAY ON NARRATIVE PERSPECTIVE

Consider the famous opening sentence of *Pride and Prejudice*: "It is a truth universally acknowledged, that a single man in possession of a good fortune must be in want of a wife." The narrator seems to be standing outside the story, not yet observing the characters but gazing off into the middle distance for some reflections on life in general. But this impression does not last. As Mr. Bennet and "his lady" begin their dialogue, it rapidly becomes clear that the storyteller had them both in view when that opening generalization was made. It is an opinion, we find, that Mrs. Bennet would greet with a clapping of hands and little cries of joy—and one Mr. Bennet would send flying to the paradise of foolish ideas with a shaft of ridicule. The narrator ostensibly takes the responsibility for the opinion; but we see from the beginning that her observations are likely to bear an ironic relation to the views, and points of view, of her characters. This is our introduction to the quality of tough yet gentle irony that will control every page of the novel, making us feel a wonderful balance between sense and sensibility.

This artful control of over-all narrative perspective in the service of Jane Austen's irony is supported by a most subtle manipulation of point of view for the sake of the novel's unity. Even a sleepy reader of this book must be well aware, before he has read very far, that it is Elizabeth Bennet's story. But how does he know this? The title gives no clue, and Elizabeth is not the storyteller. The opening pages make it clear that the matrimonial prospects of the Bennet daughters will direct the action—but there are five daughters. True, three of them look far from promising: Mary is a pedantic bore; Lydia is an empty-headed flirt; Kitty is just empty-headed. But both Jane and Elizabeth are attractive and accomplished, and for several chapters it looks as if Jane's chances with Bingley will bring the central action into focus, with Elizabeth playing some

59

subsidiary role. How is it, then, that by the time we are quarterway through the, novel—say by the time Mr. Collins makes his celebrated proposal to Elizabeth—it has become perfectly clear that Elizabeth is the heroine of *Pride and Prejudice*, and that Jane is only a secondary character?

Partly, this is revealed by the' sheer amount of attention the storyteller pays to Elizabeth, which increases rapidly as we move through the first eighteen chapters. This, of course, is itself a function of point of view. The storyteller chooses to gaze upon Elizabeth more and more often, and for longer and longer stretches of time. But the interesting fact is that this deliberate restriction of the narrator's privilege of gazing anywhere and everywhere is most stringently applied when the mechanics of the plot call, quite on the contrary, for attention to Jane. In chapter vii, Jane goes to visit Caroline Bingley at Netherfield. Mrs. Bennet's most sanguine hopes are fulfilled when Jane catches a bad cold on the way, and therefore has to spend several days with the Bingleys. But note that this is reported by letter; for when Jane leaves for Netherfield we do not go with her. The narrative perspective remains focused on the Bennet household, and particularly on Elizabeth; and it is not until Elizabeth decides to put sisterhood above gentility, and walks three miles across muddy fields, that we make our first entry into the Bingley household. Moreover, we see nothing of Jane until Elizabeth goes upstairs to nurse her; and even then we get a scanty glimpse, since Jane evidently is too sick to talk. By this time it begins to be obvious that the narrator is only slightly more interested in Jane than is the feline Miss Bingley, who tolerates her chiefly for the sake of Bingley's interest. Jane's relation to Bingley will be important in the plot, but much less for itself than as a necessary device to help build up Elizabeth's prejudice against Darcy.

(...)

Two other points about Jane Austen's management of narrative perspective repay study. One has to do with what could be called her "kinaesthetics"—the sense of movement imparted by the author to the story, and the way in which this sense is controlled; the other, closely related, is her selectivity.

Much of *Pride and Prejudice* moves at the pace of life itself: the action is rendered with a degree of detail and fullness of dialogue that gives a highly developed dramatic illusion. But note how fast the storyteller can shift to drastic synopsis when it seems desirable to step up the action and move on to a scene essential to to the plot. When Elizabeth is waiting at Longbourn for the Gardiners to come and take her on a tour of the Lake district, she is disappointed by a letter saying that they cannot start until two weeks later than planned, and consquently cannot go so far on their trip. Our shrewd narrator, however, has no intention of making us impatient without a purpose, and disposes of a whole month in two swift sentences: "Four weeks were to pass away before her uncle and aunt's arrival. But they did pass away, and Mr. and Mrs. Gardiner with their four children did at length appear at Longbourn." Geographical setting is dealt with just as jauntily: "It is not the object of this work," we are told a few lines further, "to give a description of Derbyshire, nor of any of the remarkable places through which their route thither lay. Oxford, Blenheim, Warwick, Kenilworth, Birmingham, etc., are sufficiently known." And just two pages later we are treading the plush carpets at Pemberley, ready for the next encounter between Elizabeth and Darcy.

When it comes to selectivity, the filters through which the narrator of *Pride and Prejudice* habitually views the action are much more discriminating than those of any photographer, and they positively cut out much that is the stock in trade of the average novelist. What color is Elizabeth's hair? What did she wear at the Netherfield ball? What in the world do these people eat at all the dinners that are mentioned? What do Mr. and Mrs. Bennet look like? But the answers to these and a hundred similar questions it is the narrator's privilege to withhold: we must take what he (or she) chooses to give us. What Jane Austen chooses to give is pretty well summed up in her observation about Darcy and Elizabeth at the happy moment when Elizabeth finally accepts Darcy's hand: "They walked on, without knowing in what direction. There was too much to be thought and felt and said for attention to any other objects." Thought and feeling, and their verbal expression— this is the world of Jane Austen, so beautifully illuminated for us by her artistic control of narrative perspective.

STUART TAVE ON "AFFECTION"

The form in which domestic felicity comes to Elizabeth and Darcy is unusual and it is there not by luck. It comes, first, because both are amiable and that is a necessary foundation, but it comes because on that is built something more. Above all, as Elizabeth knows, there must be love, or to use the word Jane Austen prefers in such contexts, there must be "affection." It is the quieter, more general word, for an emotion of slower growth and more lasting therefore; but it is, in this context, a strong word for a deep emotion.

(...)

The validity of the marriage between Darcy and Elizabeth is established by the time in which their affection grows, and by the capacity of the affection to withstand and to be strengthened by the proofs of time and crisis. Elizabeth is certain that the immediate effect of Lydia's disgrace will be that her own power with Darcy must sink, that everything must sink under such a proof of family weakness; it makes her understand her own wishes, and never has she so honestly felt how much she could have loved him as now when all love is vain. The whole of their acquaintance, as she can now review it, has been full of contradictions and varieties and she sighs at the perverseness of her own feelings, which have so changed. In the mode of romance Elizabeth's change is unreasonable or unnatural in comparison with the regard that arises on a first interview and even before two words have been exchanged; but she had given "somewhat of a trial" to this "method" with Wickham and its ill-success might perhaps authorize her to try the other "less interesting mode of attachment." The ironic language sounds like the language of experimental method, and it is that, in the sense of tested experience of common life as opposed to romantic prejudice, but the reality here is the reality of tried emotions. "If gratitude and esteem are good foundations of affection"—and the hypothesis has been tried by Elizabeth's mind and emotions—then the change of sentiment will be "neither improbable nor faulty" (279).

SANDRA M. GILBERT AND SUSAN GUBAR ON WOMEN IN AUSTEN

Austen's propriety is most apparent in the overt lesson she sets out to teach in all of her mature novels. Aware that male superiority is far more than a fiction, she always defers to the economic, social, and political power of men as she dramatizes how and why female survival depends on gaining male approval and protection. All the heroines who reject inadequate fathers are engaged in a search for better, more sensitive men who are, nevertheless, still the representatives of authority. As in *Northanger Abbey*, the happy ending of an Austen novel occurs when the girl becomes a daughter to her husband, an older and wiser man who has been her teacher and her advisor, whose house can provide her with shelter and sustenance and at least derived status, reflected glory. Whether it be parsonage or ancestral mansion, the man's house is where the heroine can retreat from both her parents' inadequacies and the perils of the outside world: like Henry Tilney's Woodston, Delaford, Pemberley, Donwell, and Thornton Lacy are spacious, beautiful places almost always supplied with the loveliest fruit trees and the prettiest prospects. Whereas becoming a man means proving or testing oneself or earning a vocation, becoming a woman means relinquishing achievement and accommodating oneself to men and the spaces they provide.

Dramatizing the necessity of female submission for female survival, Austen's story is especially flattering to male readers because it describes the taming not just of any woman but specifically of a rebellious, imaginative girl who is amorously mastered by a sensible man. No less than the blotter literally held over the manuscript on her writing desk, Austen's cover story of the necessity for silence and submission reinforces women's subordinate position in patriarchal culture. Interestingly, what common law called "coverture" at this time actually defined the married woman's status as suspended or "covered": "the very being or legal existence of the woman is suspended during the marriage," wrote Sir William Blackstone, "or at least is incorporated and consolidated into that of the husband under whose wing, protection and cover, she performs everything."[20] The happiest ending envisioned by Austen, at least until her very last novel, accepts the necessity of protection and cover for heroines who wish to perform anything at all.

At the same time, however, we shall see that Austen herself "performs everything" under this cover story. As Virginia Woolf noted, for all her "infallible discretion," Austen always stimulates her readers "to supply what is not there."[21] A story as sexist as that of the taming of the shrew, for example, provides her with a "blotter" or socially acceptable cover for expressing her own self-division. Undoubtedly a useful acknowledgment of her own ladylike submission and her acquiescence to masculine values, this plot also allows Austen to consider her own anxiety about female assertion and expression, to dramatize her doubts about the possibility of being both a woman and a writer. She describes both her own dilemma and, by extension, that of all women who experience themselves as divided, caught in the contradiction between their status as human beings and their vocation as females.

(...)

Pride and Prejudice (1813) continues to associate the perils of the imagination with the pitfalls of selfhood, sexuality, and assertion. Elizabeth Bennet is her father's favorite daughter because she has inherited his wit. She is talkative, satirical, quick at interpreting appearances and articulating her judgments, and so she too is contrasted to a sensible silent sister, Jane, who is quiet, unwilling to express her needs or desires, supportive of all and critical of none. While moral Jane remains an invalid, captive at the Bingleys, her satirical sister Elizabeth walks two miles along muddy roads to help nurse her. While Jane visits the Gardiners only to remain inside their house waiting hopelessly for the visitors she wishes to receive, Elizabeth travels to the Collins' establishment where she visits Lady Catherine. While Jane remains at home, lovesick but uncomplaining, Elizabeth accompanies the Gardiners on a walking tour of Derbyshire. Jane's docility, gentleness, and benevolence are remarkable, for she suffers silently throughout the entire plot, until she is finally set free by her Prince Charming.

Notes

20. Sir William Blackstone, *Commentaries of the Laws of England, Book The First* (Oxford, 1765), p. 442.

21. Woolf, "Jane Austen," pp. 142, 146.

TONY TANNER ON DEFINING "LOVE"

As we have mentioned, Jane Austen is particularly suspicious of the immediacy of sexual attraction. It is worth asking, then, what is 'love' as it emerges from the book? And we should notice first that, if Jane Austen's society minimises the bodily dimension, so it does the possibility of a transcendental one. Her concern is with conduct, almost never with religious experience. (Gilbert Ryle points out in his interesting essay 'Jane Austen and the Moralists' (which appears in *Critical Essays on Jane Austen*, ed. B.C. Southam) in which he argues that Shaftesbury's ideas influenced Jane Austen's ethics—aesthetics, that, while she often uses the word 'Mind', she almost never uses the word 'soul'.) Her society is secular and materialistic, and the terms need not be pejorative. It was a society which valued objects and the actual edifices which made up its structure; it was quite capable of sustaining a fairly nominal or unexamined piety towards the Unknown, but at its best it concentrated on how man and woman may best live in harmony with each other. (What may happen in such a society when it is not at its best, Jane Austen unsparingly reveals.) All of this obviously influenced the notion of 'love' and its relationship to marriage. Mrs Gardiner complains to Elizabeth that 'that expression of "violently in love" is so hackneyed, so doubtful, so indefinite, that it gives me very little idea', and Elizabeth duly rephrases her reading of Bingley's attitude towards Jane as a 'promising inclination'. Early in the book Charlotte and Elizabeth discuss the conscious strategies that a woman must deploy to secure the attachment of a man, and Charlotte of course demonstrates the complete triumph of conscious calculation over spontaneous emotion by her decision to marry Mr Collins. She admits that she is 'not romantic' and asks only for 'a comfortable home'. Of course Mr Collins's company is 'irksome', but in her eyes the state of marriage, as a 'preservative from want', is much more important than the actual man who makes up the marriage. As Elizabeth realises when she sees them married, Charlotte will survive by having recourse to selective inattention, deriving satisfaction from the house and screening out as far as possible the man who provided it. Elizabeth's spontaneous reaction when told of their coming marriage is, 'Impossible', but her remark is not only indecorous: it is excessive. In such a society, the need for an 'establishment' is a very real one, and in putting prudence before passion Charlotte is only doing what the economic realities of her society—as Jane Austen makes abundantly clear—all but force her to do.

Indeed passion, as such, is hardly differentiated from folly in the terms of the book. Lydia's elopement is seen as thoughtless and foolish and selfish, rather than a *grande passion*; while Mr Bennet's premature captivation by Mrs Bennet's youth and beauty is 'imprudence'. This is a key word. Mrs Gardiner warns Elizabeth against becoming involved with the impoverished Wickham, yet when it seems he will marry a Miss King for her money she describes him as 'mercenary'. As Elizabeth asks, 'what is the difference in matrimonial affairs, between the mercenary motive and the prudent motive?' Elizabeth will simply not accept Charlotte's solution as a model of true 'prudence', nor will we. There must be something between that kind of prudence and her father's imprudence. And one of the things the book sets out to do is to define a rationally based 'mode of attachment'—something between the exclusively sexual and the entirely mercenary. Thus words such as 'gratitude' and 'esteem' are used to describe Elizabeth's growing feeling for Darcy. She comes to feel that their union would have been 'to the advantage of both: by her ease and liveliness, his mind might have softened, his manners improved; and from his judgement, information, and knowledge of the world, she must have received benefit of greater importance'. A word to note there is 'advantage': consciousness has penetrated so far into emotions that love follows calculations and reflections. What differentiates Elizabeth's choice from Charlotte's is not its greater impetuosity—indeed, it is Charlotte who is the more precipitate. It is the fact that it is a free choice which is not dictated by economic pressure (though Pemberley is a great attraction, as she readily admits); and it is a choice which is based on more awareness, knowledge, and intelligence than Charlotte brings to her cool but instant capitulation. Elizabeth loves for the best reasons, and there are always reasons for loving in Jane Austen's world. Consider this sentence from Tolstoy's *Resurrection*: 'Nekhludov's offer of marriage was based on generosity and knowledge of what had happened in the past, but Simonson loved her as he found her; *he loved her simply because he loved her*' (emphasis added). Tolstoy takes in a far wider world than Jane Austen, both socially and emotionally. He knew that there are feelings of such intensity, directness and tenacity that they reduce language to tautology when it attempts to evoke them. The kind of emotion pointed to in the remarkable clause I have emphasised—not to be confused with lust, for this is far from being a purely sexual attraction—is a kind of emotion which is not conceived of, or taken into account, in Jane Austen's world. This is not to censure Jane

Austen for blinkered vision. It is, rather, to point out that in her books, and thus in the society they reflect, emotion is either rational—capable of being both conceptualised and verbalised—or it is folly.

LAURA G. MOONEYHAM ON DARCY AND ELIZABETH AS HERO AND HEROINE

The secret of *Pride and Prejudice*'s popularity lies in the dynamics between its hero and heroine. The spark of their relationship depends on their equality of intelligence and perception, for Elizabeth and Darcy are more fully equal in this sense than any other of Austen's protagonists. Each is both protagonist and antagonist; that is, their struggle is as much against each other as it is against the pressures of society or family. The novel presents a balance of power not only between two characters but between two conflicting modes of judgment, and, by extension, between two conflicting systems of language which both reflect and shape these judgments.[1] *Pride and Prejudice* resolves these conflicts in a compromise; Darcy and Elizabeth both change, though in different directions. Furthermore, in *Pride and Prejudice*, the resolution of the romance does not hinge on the capitulation of either lover to the other, as it does in some other Austen novels. For instance, in *Northanger Abbey*, Catherine Morland resolves to think and judge as Henry Tilney does. Edmund comes round to Fanny at the end of *Mansfield Park*, acknowledging his past errors and Fanny's wisdom; the heroine of *Emma* renounces her role as imaginist and binds herself to Mr. Knightley. And in *Persuasion*, Wentworth finds at the novel's conclusion that he owes his happiness less to his own efforts than to Anne's. However, at the end of *Pride and Prejudice*, though both lovers gallantly assume a more than equal share of the blame, the true portion of responsibility for their initial misery and later happiness is in equilibrium. Equality of errors leads to equality of education.

Pride and Prejudice is also the only one of Austen's novels which owes its central structure to the relationship between hero and heroine. The actions of the hero in the other five novels are of secondary importance to the design of plot. The architecture of *Northanger Abbey* is determined by the two stages of Catherine's education, by her learning the pitfalls of verbal language at Bath and written language at the Abbey. *Sense and Sensibility*'s structure is determined by the dialectic of Elinor's sense opposed to Marianne's sensibility. *Mansfield Park* is organized around Fanny as an isolated figure among public scenes of general folly—Sotherton, the theatre, the ball, Portsmouth—while the sexual dynamics between herself and Edmund are left almost wholly unexplored. In *Emma*, the structure depends upon the stages of Emma's progress from error to understanding; Mr. Knightley's and Emma's mutual attraction remains a sub-text, ever-present but not the subject of narrative focus until Emma herself acknowledges her feelings midway through Volume III. The relationship between Anne and Wentworth is central to *Persuasion*, but even here structure is determined by Anne's displacement from Kellynch and her changing status from distanced observer to central participant in the action.[2] But in *Pride and Prejudice*, the structure is a product of the relationship between Elizabeth and Darcy. The novel's pace is characterized by a rising intensity when Elizabeth and Darcy are together, and a lull, a sense of intermission, when they are apart. Since the structure results from the dynamics of attraction and antagonism between hero and heroine, it is appropriate that Darcy's first proposal to Elizabeth marks almost the exact centre of the novel. Thus *Pride and Prejudice* in its first half chronicles the growing consequences of those vices in Darcy and Elizabeth which form its title, moves at its centre to the open expression of pride and prejudice in a love scene gone desperately sour, and in its second half traces the resolution of this disunion, the compromises made in the name of love.

The structural stability of *Pride and Prejudice* also relies on the treatment of language. The first half of the novel displays the growing linguistic divisions between Elizabeth and Darcy as each perceives reality according to his or her own habit of speech—Elizabeth through wit and its attendant blindness,

Darcy through the language of reserve and privilege. When, at midpoint in the novel Darcy proposes, these two systems of language and thought clash openly for the first time. Neither Elizabeth nor Darcy hold anything back in this scene, for in the heat of anger reticence evaporates. The many months of prior misunderstanding on either side are swept away in accusation and counter-accusation. Darcy's letter, which follows the next day, supplies all missing information but does so in the rhetoric of injured pride. From this central point of aired grievances and angry honesty, Elizabeth and Darcy reconstitute a language, building their romance in the process. Darcy must discard much of his stiffness and reserve; he must recognize that others beside himself have the right to be proud. For her part, Elizabeth must suffer an isolated and silent penance because open communication with her usual confidantes— Charlotte, Jane and Mrs. Gardiner—is rendered difficult or impossible by varying circumstances. During this period of her education, Elizabeth learns to temper her wit by a more careful internal evaluation of her own feelings. The precise articulation of each stage in her changing feelings for Darcy is crucial for Elizabeth's emotional and linguistic maturation because it betokens her new respect for language as a mode of judgment.[3] Darcy too has benefited from an enforced period of meditation, for at the end of the novel we find that his period of reevaluation, analysis and regret has run parallel to Elizabeth's own. Just as Elizabeth soon memorizes Darcy's letter through sheer dint of rereading and contemplation, so too has Darcy remembered Elizabeth's angry words verbatim through the months of their separation, and has found in them a fund for meditation and self-excoriation. In this period of mutual education, Elizabeth relinquishes the language of prejudice, Darcy, the language of pride.

Notes

1. See Lionel Trilling: 'The great charm ... of *Pride and Prejudice* is that it permits us to conceive of morality as style. The relation of

Elizabeth Bennet to Darcy is real, is intense, but it expresses itself as a conflict and reconciliation of styles: a formal rhetoric, traditional and vigorous, must find a way to accommodate a female vivacity, which in turn must recognize the principled demands of the strict male syntax. The high moral import of the novel lies in the fact that the union of styles is accomplished without injury to either lover', *The Opposing Self* (New York: Viking Press, 1955), p. 222.

    2. R.S. Crane notes that 'the plot ... centers on [Anne] rather than in her and Wentworth conjointly: in what she does ... merely by being herself, to draw Wentworth gradually back to her; and in what she undergoes meanwhile in her private thoughts', 'Jane Austen: *Persuasion*' in his *The Idea of the Humanities* (University of Chicago Press, 1967), p. 290.

    3. See Reuben A. Brower, 'Light and Bright and Sparkling: Irony and Fiction in *Pride and Prejudice*' in *Jane Austen*, ed. Watt, p. 74.

ANITA G. GORMAN ON DESCRIPTIONS OF ELIZABETH BENNET'S APPEARANCE

In *Pride and Prejudice* Austen uses the reactions of other characters to describe her heroine. This method correlates with the major theme of the book perception and misperception. We may know that Elizabeth Bennet has fine eyes, but we do not know their color except that they are dark—brown, presumably—and therefore conform to the Lavaterian stereotype for heroines. We also know that Darcy was not impressed with Elizabeth's looks the first time he saw her; although Bingley calls her "pretty," Darcy will only allow her to be "tolerable." His reaction reflects Darcy's hauteur and bias against those of lower station than his. It is likely also that Elizabeth is not a dazzling beauty and that one message of the book is the value of the total person, the value of wit, vivaciousness, and intelligence over physical appearance alone.

Whereas Elizabeth is only tolerable when Darcy first meets her, the next time they meet he is attracted by those "dark eyes" (*PP* 23). Although Darcy does not know what attracts him to Elizabeth, "part of the attraction is surely a sense of her vitality, of a freedom and ultimately of a sexual energy unknown in his formal and insipid circle that entices him against his judgment"

(Chandler 35). If the eyes, as has been traditionally believed, are the windows of the soul, then Elizabeth's fine eyes symbolize the excellence of her inner nature.

Initially the perfectionist and judge who wants females to live up to some unrealizable ideal, Darcy, the narrator writes, also has to compromise: "Though he had detected with a critical eye more than one failure of perfect symmetry in her form, he was forced to acknowledge her figure to be light and pleasing..." (*PP* 23). At first, Darcy is forced by Bingley to look at Elizabeth, then to judge her; and later, he looks at her again, this time judging her more positively, and within moments he tells Caroline Bingley, who has been criticizing those in attendance, that he has been "'meditating on the very great pleasure which a pair of fine eyes in the face of a pretty woman can bestow'" (*PP* 27). Alice Chandler believes that Elizabeth's eyes become a point of contention between Darcy and Miss Bingley, because Caroline understands the potency of Darcy's interest, although she "too is unconscious of its real origins, the source of her rival's power" (35).

When Caroline Bingley asserts that no painter could capture Elizabeth's exquisite eyes, Darcy replies that it would be difficult to "'catch their expression, but their colour and shape, and the eye-lashes, so remarkably fine, might be copied'" (PP 53), implying not only that Elizabeth's physical features could be copied, but also that they should be. This section confirms Caroline Bingley's malice and Fitzwilliam Darcy's interest (he even notices eyelashes!) and functions as another comment on portrait painting. Jane Austen, it seems, was sensitive to what portrait painting can and cannot do. In *Emma*, she was to use Emma's watercolor of Harriet Smith to depict Emma's own character and to show, by means of various reactions to the portrait, the characters of Elton, Knightley, and Harriet herself. In *Pride and Prejudice*, the use of portrait painting is more indirect. But in this scene it is apparent that Mr. Darcy's remarks highlight the difference between the outer and the inner person, between the physical body and the ineffable center, that unique quality that makes an individual herself. A painter could get the dimensions and shape of her eyes but not "their expression," and from whence does their expression derive if not from the inner person, the spirit, the very identity of the individual? Darcy's remarks not only show the divergence between the physical and the "spiritual" but also his own love for Elizabeth, and his consciousness of her as a mysterious, unique individual.

Caroline Bingley's views on Elizabeth Bennet, of whom she is profoundly jealous, cannot be trusted, but the fact that she imputes certain characteristics to Elizabeth gives us indirect clues to contemporary standards of beauty. Miss Bingley complains that Elizabeth's face is "'too thin,'" her complexion not brilliant, her features "'not at all handsome,'" her nose wanting in "'character; there is nothing marked in its lines'" (*PP* 271). Miss Bingley even reports on Elizabeth's teeth, declaring that they are "'tolerable, but not out of the common way ...'" (*PP* 271). Miss Bingley's final comments about Elizabeth's eyes, that they have a "sharp, shrewish look" are not to be given credence, for we have Darcy's contrasting opinion that they are "fine" as well as Caroline's own assertion but a few minutes earlier that no painter could capture those fine eyes. Caroline's remarks in this section begin with fairly innocuous criticisms and insincere compliments, but rise to a crescendo of nastiness, revealing little about Elizabeth's appearance and a great deal about Caroline Bingley's jealousy. Finally, brashly recalling to Darcy his remark that Elizabeth is no more a beauty than her mother a wit, Miss Bingley is being deliberately cruel, and she deserves the set-down she gets from Mr. Darcy when he tells her that for a long time he has considered Elizabeth Bennet one of the best looking women he knows. Beauty exists in the eye of the beholder, when the beholder loves; ugliness also exists in the eye of the beholder, when she hates.

ANNE CRIPPEN RUDERMAN ON MR. DARCY'S VIRTUES

Austen does not hide the fact that there is a somewhat unsocial aspect to Mr. Darcy's virtue: his motive is not to make himself agreeable. It is almost always assumed by critics of *Pride and Prejudice* that Mr. Darcy represents society, and Elizabeth is a champion of individualism.[6] Before considering Mr. Darcy's asocial side, it is helpful to look at Elizabeth's sociability. That Elizabeth is lively and playful does not mean she is not respectful of social standards. Mr. Bingley's jealous sisters accuse her of "conceited independence, a most country town indifference to decorum" (36) and of a "self-sufficiency without fashion, which is intolerable" (271), insults which sound more like praise. Elizabeth does not have the fashions of the city. Her tastes and manners are rustic: she quotes a country saying about porridge, she considers pigs in the garden more interesting than a visit by Lady Catherine, she prefers a plain dish to a ragout (24, 35, 158). Mr. Darcy admires the brilliancy that country air and exercise give to her looks (33, 36). Elizabeth has the "sturdy independence of ... country customs" that Mary Crawford makes fun of in *Mansfield Park* (58). Just as *Mansfield Park* presents Mary's city tastes and education as connected to her lack of real principle, we should not be surprised to find in *Pride and Prejudice* that country independence is a sign of sturdiness of conviction, including a respect not for fashion but for propriety.

Elizabeth is an unreliable narrator, and her statements about herself must be weighed against her actions. She claims to love to laugh at people: "follies and nonsense, whims and inconsistencies do divert me, I own, and I laugh at them whenever I can" (57). Such statements have led to a general perception of her as a detached observer.[7] But in truth she *fails* to laugh at a surprising number of things. She has no delight in the absurdities of Sir William Lucas for she has known them too long (152), she is not diverted by the evening entertainment at Lady Catherine's but only finds it "superlatively stupid" (166). That she is not as detached as her father is clear when Mr. Bingley abandons Jane. Elizabeth listens "in silent indignation" (133) while Mr. Bennet only laughs, saying "a girl likes to be crossed in love a little now and then" (137).

Elizabeth's own manners, if not fashionable, are reserved.

She dismisses the waiter when her sister begins to talk about Wickham, and Lydia says the action "is just like your formality and discretion" (220). When Elizabeth gets home after Lydia has eloped, she asks whether there is "a servant belonging to it, who did not know the whole story" and Jane must explain how difficult it is to be guarded at such a time (292). Elizabeth does not need Mr. Darcy to point out the improprieties of her own family: at a ball, for example, she is "deeply ... vexed," feels "inexpressible vexation," and finally "blushed and blushed again with shame and vexation" at her family (98–100). She is "in agonies" over her sister Mary's pedantic singing and then regrets her father's improper way of putting an end to it (100–101). She is clearly not, like her father, enjoying this display of folly (103). As usual, Jane Austen leaves an ambiguity about Elizabeth's motives, for while her shame attests to her respect for propriety it also reveals her unacknowledged wish for Mr. Darcy's good opinion. That Elizabeth laughs "when she can" does not indicate her indifference to society but rather her attempt not to "increase her vexations, by dwelling on them" (232). Elizabeth's pursuit of happiness means that she makes the best of things, and must make us wonder if she really is "the outspoken champion of ... individual desire."[8]

As for Mr. Darcy, from the first we see not that he has great respect for social conventions but rather that he does not always observe social rules. The servile and self-important Mr. Collins strictly adheres to the forms of civility: his manners are "very formal" (64, 107, 155) and "solemn" (66, 90, 105), his formality is marked by his incessant gratitude and apologies. Mr. Darcy is never apologetic and is disliked precisely because he does not pay much attention to social forms, such as making polite conversation or asking an unattached girl to dance (see 10–19). This indifference to social opinion exposes him to ridicule. Elizabeth, although hardly endeared to Mr. Darcy by his refusal to dance with her, can find his action "ridiculous" instead of upsetting (12), for it indicates that he does not know (or care) what social rules require. Even his friends laugh at his aloofness (11, 51, 55, 175, 180). Just as his neighbors assume he is contemptuous of them, so they assume he cannot be laughed at. Elizabeth, for example, several times *thinks* "she could perceive he was rather offended" and therefore checks her laugh (51, cf. 57, 371), but there is no real evidence that she is right.

In fact, Austen indicates that Mr. Darcy's behavior is not due to a general contempt of his social inferiors but rather to his virtue. Unlike less worthy men, he is not motivated by a desire to be liked by others. Austen, as usual—and contrary to common opinion about her[9]—suggests that good manners are *not* always a sign of virtue: Mr. Darcy, for example, is "sure of giving offense" everywhere (16). Mr. Darcy is unyielding and determined (324, cf. 58) and capable of anger (73, 94, 190): good manners involve a softening of all these traits. (This is why Hobbes attacks the Darcys of the world.) Elizabeth reflects that if she married Mr. Darcy, "by her ease and liveliness, his mind might have been *softened*, his manners improved" (312, emphasis added). To be lively is what, Mrs. Gardiner says, "if he marry prudently, his wife may teach him" (325). It is Elizabeth who will socialize Mr. Darcy, not the other way around.

Austen is always somewhat suspicious of inviting manners, for she recognizes that virtue has a hard and even disagreeable side. We are allowed to compare Mr. Darcy not only to the servile Mr. Collins but also to the more charming Mr. Bingley and Mr. Wickham, just as in *Emma* the somewhat harsh Mr. Knightley is contrasted to the more agreeable Mr. Churchill. Now, Austen gives agreeableness its due. A talent at conversation is a part of good breeding, when it is used to put others at ease. Mr. Bingley has a captivating ease (9, 10, 14, 15, 16) that makes others like him. Colonel Fitzwilliam "entered into conversation directly with the readiness and ease of a well-bred man" (171), and the endeavors of Miss Darcy's companion "to introduce some kind of discourse, proved her to be more truly well bred" than Mr. Bingley's sisters (267). Mr. Darcy claims he does not have the "talent" of "conversing easily with those I have never seen before" (175). He cannot "catch their tone" or "appear interested in their concerns," he says, and Elizabeth and Colonel Fitzwilliam seem right to point out that this is because he won't take the trouble. His manners suffer for his high-mindedness and self-sufficiency.

Austen never suggests that all good things go together. She does not defend Mr. Darcy (or Mr. Knightley, similar in this respect) on the score of agreeableness, but she does defend their virtue. And to some extent she discounts the importance of inviting manners. There is a fine line between using conversation to make others feel more comfortable and using it to call attention to one's own ease. When Emma says her idea of Frank Churchill is "that he can adapt his conversation to the taste of everybody" (E 150) (here she echoes the foolish Mrs. Bennet, whose idea of good breeding is to have "always something to say to everybody" [PP 44]) Mr. Knightley exclaims that, if so, he will be insufferable: "What! at three-and-twenty to be the king of his company ... to make everybody's talents conduce to the display of his own superiority" (E 150). In Mr. Wickham, we see how good manners are self-serving. Even after Elizabeth understands Wickham's real character, she can still admit that

> his manners were always so pleasing, that had his character and his marriage been exactly what they ought, his smiles and his easy address ... would have delighted them all (PP 316).

Wickham's "vicious propensities" are not signaled by his manners but are only visible to one who "had opportunities of seeing him in unguarded moments" (200). The problem is that the deepest vanity can most master social graces: the Bertram sisters are among those whose "vanity is in such good order that they seemed quite free from it" (MP 35).

Notes

6. Samuel Kliger, in a defense of this thesis, says that "Darcy is the spokesman for civilization" while Elizabeth represents "man-in-nature." (See Kliger, "Jane Austen's *Pride and Prejudice* in the Eighteenth-Century Mode" in *Twentieth Century Interpretations of Pride and Prejudice*, ed. E. Rubinstein [Englewood Cliffs, N.J.: Prentice–Hall, Inc., 1969],

53–54.) Tanner (*Jane Austen*, 136) similarly sees Elizabeth as the "freely rambling individual" and Darcy as the "rigidified upholder of the group" and their marriage as bringing together these principles. For similar ideas see also Litz, *Jane Austen*, 104–105; Nardin, *Those Elegant Decorums*, 60–61; Duckworth, *The Improvement*, 118; Mordecai Marcus, *Twentieth-Century Interpretations*, Rubinstein, 84; and Poovey, *The Proper Lady*, 189, 201.

7. See, for example, Morgan, who argues that Elizabeth's freedom is "a freedom to keep from becoming involved" and that she, like her father, refuses to commit her intelligence to seriousness and to a moral life (Morgan, *In the Meantime*, 83–92). See also Butler, who agrees with most critics that Elizabeth is fearless and independent and finds her similar to her father in her misanthropy (Butler, *Jane Austen and the War*, 199, 210). Elizabeth's tendencies to be vexed at people seem to me precisely to indicate her involvement with the world and to distinguish her from her father, who never gets upset and is hardly ever annoyed. The more foolish his acquaintances, the more he likes them (e.g., 68, 213, 364).

8. Mary Poovey, *The Proper Lady*, 194. See also Johnson who argues that in *Pride and Prejudice* "pursuing happiness is the business of life" and that Elizabeth has "a philosophy of pleasure" (C. Johnson, *Jane Austen*, 78, 80). The examples discussed above suggest that in Jane Austen's novels, pursuing happiness and hedonism are not the same.

9. See, for example, Nardin, who says that in *Pride and Prejudice*, if "a man or woman always displays good manners, it is perfectly safe for the reader to assume that his character is truly good" (Nardin, *Those Elegant Decorums*, 47).

JULIET MCMASTER ON MR. BENNET AND ELIZABETH BENNET

Mr. Bennet is Jane Austen's Walter Shandy, a man with a set of hobby-horses, mental constructs that he has substituted for the reality that surrounds him. His feelings are seldom described, but his mental operations have the force of passions. His attitude is carefully accounted for. We are to suppose that since his emotional life has been a disaster, he has retreated to a cerebral irony, whereby all the troubles and disappointments of life are to be viewed as mere amusements. His "conjugal felicity," by the time we know the Bennets, has been reduced to the kind of satisfaction we see him deriving from his verbal barbs at his wife's expense in the first scene.

To his wife he was very little otherwise indebted, than as her ignorance and folly had contributed to his amusement. This is not the sort of happiness which a man would in general wish to owe to his wife; but where other powers of entertainment are wanting, the true philosopher will derive benefit from such as are given. (236)

Like Walter, another "true philosopher," he can even contemplate the death of a child with equanimity, as long as it gives him the opportunity for a *bon mot*. "Well, my dear," he tells Mrs. Bennet when the news comes that Jane is confined at Netherfield, after being sent out in the rain to dine with the Bingleys, "if your daughter should have a dangerous fit of illness, if she should die, it would be a comfort to know that it was all in pursuit of Mr. Bingley, and under your orders" (31). He has deliberately set aside the natural preference of a father for his offspring, in favour of a clinical lack of bias: "If my children are silly I must hope to be always sensible of it," he announces coolly (29). There is a searing quality about his wit and his lack of compassion. In the face of Jane's genuine unhappiness when Bingley abandons her, he can respond only with the critical satisfaction of a spectator at a play: "Next to being married, a girl likes to be crossed in love a little now and then. It is something to think of, and gives her a sort of distinction among her companions" (137–8).

He can successfully separate his personal interest from his aesthetic appreciation of Wickham's roguery when he considers the matter of the price Wickham sets on himself as a husband for Lydia: "Wickham's a fool, if he takes her with a farthing less than ten thousand pounds. I should be sorry to think so ill of him, in the very beginning of our relationship" (304). For Mr. Bennet is a connoisseur, a spectator and a critic of the kind dear to Browning and James. "For what do we live, but to make sport for our neighbours, and laugh at them in our turn?" he asks, not expecting an answer (364). Such a question looks forward to Ralph Touchett's in *The Portrait of a Lady*: "What's the use of being ill and disabled and restricted to mere spectatorship at the game of life if I really can't see the show when I've paid so much for my ticket?" (ch. 15) Mr. Bennet's stance of intellectual detachment is sometimes exposed almost as a negation of itself, a moral idiocy. As in *Love and Freindship*, where acute sensibility to the pains of others is finally shown to be an elaborate kind of selfishness, in *Pride and Prejudice* we see Mr. Bennet's wit and acuity as a kind of obtuseness. When he tries to share a joke about the rumour of Darcy's courtship with Elizabeth, even she, his disciple, is unable to participate: "It was necessary to laugh, when she would rather have cried. Her father had most cruelly mortified her, ... and she could do nothing but wonder at such a want of penetration" (364).

The judgement on Mr. Bennet for neglecting his responsibilities as husband and father is clear enough, but the reader is very ready to forgive him. For it is in large measure the sins of Mr. Bennet and his favourite daughter, their overweening intelligence and relish for the absurd, that make *Pride and Prejudice* such delightful reading. He in particular is our on-stage spectator and critic, articulating and sometimes creating for us our delight in the people and incidents around him. Mr. Collins in himself is a fine creation, but it is Mr. Collins as savoured and drawn out by Mr. Bennet who becomes immortal.

Elizabeth, to her lasting glory, has style, and much of her style is an inheritance from her father. "She had a lively, playful disposition," we hear at the outset, "which delighted in any thing ridiculous" (12). In fact, so far as she is one of the Quixotes in Jane Austen's novels, she behaves not so much according to the model of romance as according to the model set by her father. It is because she wants to live up to her position as his favourite daughter that she means to be clever. After she has read and absorbed Darcy's letter, and so come to know herself, she is able to recognize the exact nature of her failing.

I meant to be uncommonly clever in taking so decided dislike to him, without any reason. It is such a spur to one's genius, such an opening for wit to have a dislike of that kind. (225–6)

Spurs to one's genius and openings for wit are likely to be items coveted by a devoted daughter of Mr. Bennet. And as the process of Catherine Morland's and Emma's education involves their discarding romantic models of experience, so Elizabeth learns by gradually sloughing off the influence of her father's aesthetic detachment.

At the outset it is strong. She comes on as delighting in the ridiculous, she accepts the title of "a studier of character" (42) and announces "Follies and nonsense, whims and inconsistencies *do* divert me, I own, and I laugh at them whenever I can" (57). Like her father, she is a vehicle for much of the reader's appreciation in taking on the examination and elucidation of character, as she does of Bingley's and Darcy's during her stay at Netherfield. She also becomes the critic and exponent of her own character (not always a reliable one), and the traits she chooses to emphasise bear perhaps more relation to a model derived from her father than to the truth. "I always delight in overthrowing ... schemes, and cheating a person of their premeditated contempt," she tells Darcy when she expects him to despise her taste (52). It is the same delight manifested by Mr. Bennet when he refuses to call on Bingley, and subsequently visits him on the sly. To be whimsical and unpredictable is his mode also. And in her as in her father we see that interpenetration of emotional with intellectual response, so that mental operations have the force of strong feeling. "You take delight in vexing me," Mrs. Bennet accuses her husband, with unusual perspicacity (5). Similarly Elizabeth is glad to be "restored ... to the enjoyment of all her original dislike" towards the Bingley sisters (35). By a characteristic process, her emotion becomes subordinate to her consciousness of the emotion.

Elizabeth takes pains to live up to her father and share his attitudes. When Mr. Bennet is joking about Jane's being jilted,

Elizabeth enters into the spirit of his irony: at his suggestion that Wickham "would jilt you creditably," she replies, "Thank you, Sir, but a less agreeable man would satisfy me. We must not all expect Jane's good fortune" (138). She takes up his proposition in her letter to her aunt, in which she humorously announces that Wickham *has* jilted her; but here she is able to make a sensible qualification:

> I am now convinced, my dear aunt, that I have never been much in love; for had I really experienced that pure and elevating passion, I should at present detest his very name, and wish him all manner of evil. By my feelings are not only cordial towards *him*; they are even impartial towards Miss King.... There can be no love in all this. My watchfulness has been effectual; and though I should certainly be a more interesting object to all my acquaintance, were I distractedly in love with him, I cannot say that I regret my comparative insignificance. Importance may sometimes be purchased too dearly. (150)

The passage shows her propensity to snatch up an emotional subject and cunningly encase it in an intellectual web. She had been enough in love with Wickham, at one time, to have "her head full of him" (not her heart, we notice). But such emotion as she has felt is successfully analysed and dissected, and proves to have been little more than an idea, a mere opinion. Now like her father she can mock love by her parodic terminology—"that pure and elevating passion," "distractedly in love"—and presently her desertion by Wickham is imagined as a spectacle for others, wherein she is to figure as the "interesting object." However, her mental health is such that she will not be seduced by this attraction, and she sensibly concludes "Importance may sometimes be purchased too dearly." Though she was ready to participate in her father's savouring of the aesthetic pleasure in the spectacle of the jilted lady, she will not surrender her happiness in order to have the satisfaction of providing the spectacle. This is comedy, after all, and a light, bright and sparkling one at that.

Elizabeth's misjudgement of the relative merits of Darcy and Wickham is in large measure a result of her aesthetic stance. Darcy offends her by saying she is not handsome enough to tempt him; Wickham wins her allegiance by telling her a story. His version of his youth and blighted prospects has the verbal embellishment of romantic fiction:

> His estate there is a noble one.... I verily believe I could forgive him any thing and every thing, rather than his disappointing the hopes and disgracing the memory of his father.... I have been a disappointed man, and my spirits will not bear solitude. (77–9)

The satisfying fiction, along with Wickham's professional delivery, charms Elizabeth, and she believes it because she wants to. As her father takes life to be a spectacle, Elizabeth will accept a fiction as life. She leaves Wickham with her head full of him, and insists "there was truth in his looks" (86). Subsequently she is to elaborate on his story, and construct from it her own version of the fable of the virtuous and idle apprentices.

After Darcy's letter Elizabeth cannot be in concert with her father. The education about the errors of prejudice and first impressions goes with a discarding of attitudes she had imbibed from him. Some readers have seen this moral awakening as a disappointing taming of a vivacious heroine. But it is a necessary part of her detaching herself from her father and becoming her own person. Now she urges the unsuitability of Lydia's going to Brighton, and is exasperated by Mr. Bennet's irresponsible detachment. Though she "had never been blind to the impropriety of her father's behaviour as a husband," we hear it is only now that her judgement overcomes her partiality and loyalty: "she had never felt so strongly as now, the disadvantages which must attend the children of so unsuitable a marriage, nor ever been so fully aware of the evils arising from so ill judged a direction of talents" (236–7). The failure in sympathy between father and daughter persists until the final fortunate culmination. He becomes the painful reminder of her own follies by continuing to assume her "pointed dislike" of Darcy, and by his revival of her prejudice: "We all know him to be a proud, unpleasant sort of man," he says of the man she proposes to marry (376).

Of course it is not only Mr. Bennet who is to blame for his daughter's misguided following in his footsteps. Elizabeth is responsible, and very clearly elects her own path. There is an emphasis not just on her mistakes, but on her wilful choice of them. If she goes astray, she does so very consciously, even though she is unaware of the full extent of her wandering. In discussing Jane's behaviour with Charlotte, Elizabeth insists that Jane, unlike the husband-hunting girl that Charlotte posits, has no "plan," "she is not acting by design" (22). It is one more of the points of contrast between the sisters by which Jane Austen defines Elizabeth's character; for Elizabeth by contrast *is* acting by design, though to an extent she does not herself recognize. "Design" is another word that recurs in the novel with pointed frequency, and is often connected with the pattern of planned matches. Mr. Bennet asks if marrying one of the Bennet girls is Bingley's "design in settling here" (4). Wickham pursues Georgiana Darcy to Ramsgate, "undoubtedly by design" (202). Mr. Collins admits during his proposal that he came to Hertfordshire "with the design of selecting a wife" (105), and congratulates himself after his marriage that he and his wife "seem to have been designed for each other" (216). Except in the case of Jane, Elizabeth is prone to attribute "design" to others—she sees through Miss Bingley's "designs" on Darcy (170), and considers Bingley the slave of his "designing friends" (133). Less clearsightedly, she angrily accuses Darcy of proposing to her "with so evident a design of offending and insulting me" (190). But she often accuses others of faults she does not recognize in herself.

ALLISON THOMPSON ON DANCING AND BALLS IN AUSTEN'S TIME

In order to understand Austen's use of dance in her novels, let us begin with some general statements about the ballroom in the last quarter of the eighteenth century. In the 1770s, a formal Assembly in London or Bath would open with a series of minuets, the French dance for one couple at a time. The rest of the participants would sit on benches that lined the room and watch, as couple after couple would apply to the Master of Ceremonies for permission to dance.

At Bath and other towns where older people congregated, a ball would continue to be opened by at least one minuet during even the early years of the nineteenth century. The dance was definitely antiquated, even in Austen's youth, however, and none of her heroines seem to know it. Instead, they enjoy the more social country dances. Country dances had had a peculiarly English character since the publication of John Playford's *The English Dancing Master* in 1651. Dances for two, three, four or more couples at a time, they were more lively and relaxed than the complex French dances like the *minuet*, the *boure* or the *louvre*. By the late eighteenth century, most country dances were performed in a "longways" set for five to eight couples, with partners standing opposite each other.

Dances were usually performed in what are today called "triple minor longways" sets. That is, the dance began with only the first couple starting at the top and dancing with couples two and three. At the end of one turn through the dance the first couple progressed to dance with couples three and four, while couple two waited or "stood out" at the top of the set for two more turns of the dance until they, too, had an opportunity to begin dancing.

Because so many couples stood relatively passively during the dance, they used this time as a welcome opportunity to talk and flirt—as many dancing masters, who preferred attentive silence, pointed out with indignation. The dance would continue until the original first couple had worked its way back to the "top" or the beginning of the set. Couples who danced down the set but then walked away to sit down rather than performing their social duty as inactive couples working up the set were considered selfish and disrespectful.

(...)

Austen demonstrated this precept that gentlemanly behavior and style were both expressed in dancing several times. When the obsequious Sir William Lucas attempts to compliment Mr. Darcy, he says: "'I have been most highly gratified indeed, my dear Sir. Such very superior dancing is not often seen. *It is evident that you belong to the first circles*'" (*P&P* 92; emphasis added). While his words are silly and his timing poor, the expression of his gallantry would have been easily recognized by contemporary readers. Yet, by eighteenth century standards, Mr. Darcy by his haughty behavior and previous refusals to dance has amply demonstrated that he considers himself above his company. The more amiable Mr. Bingley, who "danced every dance" (10), has behaved in a more gentlemanly fashion.

(...)

At more formal or more public balls, the ladies could "draw for numbers" upon entering the ballroom. As each dance began, the Master of Ceremonies would then call out the numbers and assign the ladies and their partners to places. The topmost lady in the first set would choose the dance. This meant that a couple could ask for the specific figures associated with a specific tune, such as Bath Assembly, Trip to Tunbridge or The Duke of Kent's Waltz. It also meant that a lady could announce a group of figures that she devised herself and ask for a tune of a certain length to accompany them. At the conclusion of the dance, the Master of Ceremonies would reshuffle the sets, and a new lady would request or "call" a dance.

While this procedure may sound daunting, in any given evening, dances were probably chosen from a fairly small pool of what were considered to be the most fashionable dances for any given year. This practice was facilitated, or perhaps fostered, by the custom of music publishers to produce slim annual collections of dances, such as "Twenty Four Country Dances for the Year 17—."

These volumes all promised to include only the latest and most fashionable dances, though many of them did include reprints of earlier dances. These popular books were in fact a necessity: starting in about 1730 or so, country dances became less and less original and were attached or devised to go with a specific and easily recognizable tune. From 1730 to 1830 over twenty-seven thousand country dances with their tunes were published in England alone (Keller 8). The dances had increasingly become combinations and recombinations of a small number of figures so that the dances were not very easily differentiated from each other. Although easy to learn just by watching the top couple (a characteristic which added to their popularity), they were hard to remember. Indeed, some dancing masters found it necessary to request participants not to dance the same dance more than once in an evening—a sure sign that this proscribed behavior must have occurred frequently enough to be noticed and criticized. This very popularity of the country dance eventually contributed to its demise. Towards the end of George III's life, even the country dances were finally going out of fashion among the "smart set"; there were too many dull dances set to dull tunes and people were ready for something innovative.

Though the Regency ballroom was dominated by country dances, there were several other major categories of dance that could be seen there: the so-called "Scotch" dances, the quadrille, and the waltz. Starting in the 1780s, a wave of romantic enthusiasm for the culture of the Gaelic North swept over England. Scottish country dances were popular in England, as were the Scotch Threesome and Foursome Reels, which featured a weaving "hey" figure interspersed with points at which performers would perform showy steps. During the course of the dance the men (and occasionally) the ladies would raise one or both arms above their heads, snap their fingers together and give the distinctive yell or "heuch."

In *Pride and Prejudice* Austen shows Scotch dances twice: first at the Lucases, where a large party is assembled. After the ladies perform a few songs, and pedantic Mary bores everyone with a long concerto, she is "glad to purchase praise and gratitude by Scotch and Irish airs, at the request of her younger sisters" who, with some young officers, start dancing at one end of the room, to the indignation of Mr. Darcy (25). Later, Miss

Bingley is playing at Netherfield while Elizabeth visits due to Jane's illness. She plays a "lively Scotch air" and Mr. Darcy draws near and in a clumsy attempt to make conversation asks Elizabeth: "'Do you not feel a great inclination, Miss Bennet, to seize such an opportunity of dancing a reel?'" (52).

(...)

As should be clear by now, an assembly was more than just a dance; it was a prime area for young ladies and gentlemen to get to know each other. Young people were expected to have on hand a repertoire of light conversation, with which to pass the time during the dance while they stood inactive. Readers will remember the lengthy scene in *Pride and Prejudice* where Elizabeth forces Mr. Darcy to speak during the course of their first two dances: "'It is your turn to say something now, Mr. Darcy. *I* talked about the dance, and you ought to make some kind of remark on the size of the room, or the number of couples'" (91).

Novels, plays, and poems of the past are often fruitful sources for a dance historian to learn more about the attitudes towards or conventions of the dance. Despite the fact that Austen never describes a specific dance, her novels are particularly useful sources, as we have seen. In addition, an understanding of the conventions of the period provides today's readers with a deeper understanding of the characterizations in Jane Austen's works, as illuminated by her dance episodes.

Works Cited

Austen, Jane. *The Novels of Jane Austen*. Ed. R.W. Chapman. 3rd ed. Oxford: OUP, 1969.

Byron, Lord George. "The Waltz; An Apostrophic Hymn," from *The Poetical Works of Lord Byron*. London: Oxford UP, 1996.

Dun, Barclay. *A Translation of Nine of the Most Fashionable Quadrilles*. Edinburgh: privately printed, 1818.

Goethe, Johann Wolfgang von. *The Sufferings of Young Werther*. Trans. Elizabeth Mayer and Louis Bogan. 1774; New York: Random House, 1970.

Keller, Kate Van Winkle. *If the Company Can Do It! Technique in Eighteenth-Century American Social Dance* (Sandy Hook, Conn.: Hendrickson Group, 1990.

Wilson, Thomas. *The Address: or, An Essay on Deportment*. London: printed by the Author, 1821.

H. ELIZABETH ELLINGTON ON LANDSCAPE AND THE FILMING

Pride and Prejudice, written in the 1790s and extensively revised before its publication in 1813, is, arguably, the first of Jane Austen's novels to make extensive use of what Austen in *Mansfield Park* terms "the influence of place." According to Ann Banfield, the "influence of place" determines the development of individual characters as physical setting "interacts with and forms consciousness" (35). In *Pride and Prejudice*, this is best illustrated in what Roger Sale refers to as the "Pemberley chapters" (42), which describe Elizabeth Bennet's journey to Derbyshire with her aunt and uncle and their tour of Mr. Darcy's ancestral estate at Pemberley. As Elizabeth interacts with the landscape surrounding Darcy's home, she is, depending upon one's reading, either inspired for the first time with feelings of love for Darcy or first recognizes the feelings that she already has for him. In either reading, the physical setting of Pemberley forms Elizabeth's consciousness of her love for Darcy. As she facetiously tells her sister, Jane, who asks when Elizabeth first began to love Darcy, "I believe I must date it from my first seeing his beautiful grounds at Pemberley" (Austen 373). As Michael Riffaterre persuasively argues in *Fictional Truth*, Darcy's grounds and home symbolize their owner; the repetition of adjectives such as "large," "beautiful," and "handsome" in Austen's description of Pemberley refer not to the landscape or the house itself, but to its owner, who becomes, through his landscape and through his role as a landowner, worthy of Elizabeth's love. Landscape, in *Pride and Prejudice*, becomes the sign of desire.

Austen's use of landscape in *Pride and Prejudice* is, however, much more complex than Sale allows in his examination of the Pemberley chapters. Through landscape, Austen addresses the wider social and economic issues many critics of her fiction claim she ignores. Class issues come to the forefront in *Pride and Prejudice*: we can read the history of land transformation through enclosure and agricultural advances, the vogue for landscape gardening, as well as the growth of middle-class consumerism in the rise of domestic tourism. Austen's was an age of art about nature: connected with the agricultural revolution and the rise of domestic tourism was a new interest in looking at the land and representing landscape in paintings and poetry and in theorizing principles of Beautiful, Sublime, and Picturesque landscape. The ideas about landscape and ways of reading landscape that were current during Austen's lifetime inform all of her works. In reading *Pride and Prejudice*, we become, in effect, consumers of landscape as much as of love story.

Pride and Prejudice, easily the most visual of Austen's six completed novels, is, not coincidentally, the most frequently filmed of her works, lending itself to cinematic adaptation more readily than her other novels through its extensive use of visual imagery and language. Both the 1940 Hollywood version, adapted for the screen by Aldous Huxley and Jane Murfin and directed by Robert Z. Leonard, and the 1995 joint BBC/A&E version, scripted by Andrew Davies and directed by Simon Langton, capitalize on the "visual pleasure" of the text (Mulvey 412) and borrow many of Austen's own devices for setting scenes, such as shots divided by windows which place the spectator on the inside looking out at the scene or on the outside looking in on the scene. Langton and Davies enjoy certain advantages that Leonard and Huxley/Murfin simply did not have available to them, such as a six-hour running time and the possibility of filming on location. Landscape imagery is thus much more developed in the 1995 version. Both films, however, offer readings of Austen that, through landscape, direct our attention to or away from certain episodes, offer subtle rereadings or (perhaps) misreadings of the novel, and show us what elements of Austen's narrative were ideologically current and thus worth emphasizing in 1940 and what elements are ideologically current in the 1990s.

The films, like Austen's novel, convert the viewer/spectator into a consumer, both of pastoral English landscape and of what constitutes Englishness at a given time period. In this essay, I will focus on the ways in which our consumption of landscape as readers informs and differs from our consumption of landscape as viewers of two filmed versions of *Pride and Prejudice*. One motive behind the Huxley/Murfin production was to capitalize on the success of recent adaptations of English novels, like *Wuthering Heights* (1939), filmed as an epic of the English landscape, and *Rebecca* (1940), both starring Laurence Olivier. The England of MGM's *Pride and Prejudice*, however, is less pastoral than pugilistic. World War II, which broke out several days after Aldous Huxley began working with Jane Murfin on an adaptation of Helen Jerome's successful play based on *Pride and Prejudice* (Turan 141), colors Huxley and Murfin's conception of Austen's novel. The 1995 adaptation by Davies capitalizes on the recent spate of Austen adaptations, most of which can be read as tributes to the English countryside and nostalgia for a bygone lifestyle.

Film adaptations necessarily convert the active pleasure of reading a text to the passive pleasure of viewing an image. Laura Mulvey argues that the pleasure of cinema is, in part, scopophilic. We find pleasure in looking, and, through our identification with the characters, in being looked at (Mulvey 416). Cinematic codes, she contends, "create a gaze, a world, and an object, thereby producing an illusion cut to the measure of desire" (427). What defines cinema is "the place of the look ... the possibility of varying it and exposing it" (427). In this essay, I will be tracing "the look" as it is directed toward landscape—the gaze both of the characters within the narrative and of the viewer watching the narrative unfold in Austen and in two film versions of *Pride and Prejudice*. What visual directions does Austen give in the text? Do the filmmakers follow Austen or diverge from her in focusing our gaze on landscape and characters in landscape? What are we looking at and what does it mean for us to look at it? What kind of world and object do these filmmakers create for our gaze? How do they capitalize on British and American nostalgia for Old England? Mulvey's theories about the gaze and spectatorship, which she applies to women and to images of women in film, are equally applicable to the use of landscape and of characters, particularly women, in the landscape for adaptations of *Pride and Prejudice*. In what Mulvey and other film theorists call "Hollywood cinema," women on film are "simultaneously looked at and displayed, with their appearance coded for strong visual and erotic impact so that they can be said to connote *to-be-looked-at-ness*" (Mulvey 418): "Going far beyond highlighting a woman's to-be-looked-at-ness, cinema builds the way she is to be looked at into the spectacle itself" (427). The two versions of *Pride and Prejudice* negotiate the to-be-looked-at-ness of Austen's landscape in different ways: landscape in the Huxley/Murfin production is overshadowed by the to-be-looked-at-ness of Greer Garson as Elizabeth Bennet, while in the Davies adaptation, Jennifer Ehle as Elizabeth Bennet is superseded by the real star of the show, Old England, bucolic and gorgeous.

(...)

In the scene after Elizabeth views the Derbyshire landscape, Mrs. Gardiner persuades her to make a side trip to Pemberley, the pivotal moment in both the novel and the 1995 film. Viewing Darcy's personal environment enables Elizabeth to see through the arrogant facade he presents to Hertfordshire and to appreciate his merit and worth, which are revealed "in his aesthetic practice" of house- and groundskeeping (Duckworth 403). Austen's physical description of Pemberley is deceptively vague:

> The park was very large, and contained great variety of ground. They entered it in one of its lowest points, and drove for some time through a beautiful wood, stretching over a wide extent.
> Elizabeth's mind was too full for conversation, but she saw and admired every remarkable spot and point of view.

They gradually ascended for half a mile, and then found
themselves at the top of a considerable eminence, where
the wood ceased, and the eye was instantly caught by
Pemberley House, situated on the opposite side of a
valley, into which the road with some abruptness wound.
It was a large, handsome, stone building, standing well on
rising ground, and backed by a ridge of high woody
hills;—and in front, a stream of some natural importance
was swelled into greater, but without any artificial
appearance. Its banks were neither formal, nor falsely
adorned. Elizabeth was delighted. She had never seen a
place for which nature had done more, or where natural
beauty had been so little counteracted by an awkward
taste. They were all of them warm in their admiration;
and at that moment she felt, that to be mistress of
Pemberley might be something! [Austen 245]

What seems nonspecific in Austen—the "large, handsome"
house, the "high woody hills," the informal banks of the
stream—is, in fact, a highly detailed description of the perfect
late eighteenth-century landscape garden. Influenced by
theories of the Picturesque and the rise of landscape painting,
landowners went to great pains to conceal their houses along
the approach until a "considerable eminence" was reached
which would afford a commanding view of the property,
transforming the land and house into a picture: "This method
of landscaping inevitably demanded that the pictures thus
created be seen from ordained and fixed points of view,
connected with each other by walks thickly wooded enough to
prevent the pictures being glimpsed from anywhere except the
right place" (Barrell 47). The setting of Pemberley in the
Davies production conforms in all particulars to Barrell's
description. Situated among what Mr. Gardiner in the film calls
"woods and groves enough to satisfy even your enthusiasm for
them, Lizzy" Pemberley is reached from a long drive that
conceals all views of the house itself until the visitor is nearly
there. At this point, trees have been cleared to open a view
across the stream to the house itself, a Palladian-style

mansion. Mr. Gardiner, recognizing that this view has been created especially for him and other tourists, commands the carriage to stop so that its occupants can consume the spectacle of Pemberley, presented like a painting between the frame of trees.

Elizabeth continues her Picturesque touring even on entering the house, which does not, however, interest either her or Austen overly much; its rooms, like its exterior, are merely handsome and large.[2] Austen and Elizabeth save their attention for Darcy's "beautiful grounds" (373). Even when Elizabeth is inside the house, her attention turns to the outdoors:

> Elizabeth, after slightly surveying it [the dining-parlor], went to a window to enjoy its prospect. The hill, crowned with wood, from which they had descended, receiving increased abruptness from the distance, was a beautiful object. Every disposition of the ground was good; and she looked on the whole scene, the river, the trees scattered on its banks, and the winding of the valley, as far as she could trace it, with delight. As they passed into other rooms, these objects were taking different positions; but from every window there were beauties to be seen. [Austen 246]

The windows frame the landscape for Elizabeth, presenting her with shifting perspectives on the same scene. As she watches through windows, Pemberley's grounds become the spectacle to be consumed, a model of the Picturesque prospect. The grounds give the impression of naturalness, which Austen does not correct, but clearly the hand of man was at work to create the spectacle that is Pemberley. As Austen implies in her description of Elizabeth's first view of Pemberley, obvious artifice was unseemly; the goal of late eighteenth-century garden design was to take into account the natural characteristics of the land, in the case of Pemberley, woods and a stream, and "improve upon them by art, make [them] more beautiful by art, so that the garden would look like nature untouched by man" (Hall 108). The goal, in other words, was to swell the natural importance of the house and grounds into greater eminence, through precise prunings, plantings, and subtle ornamentation.

The most indispensable element in this kind of landscaping is land—"not simply as the raw material to be worked but as its own ornament and aesthetic effect as well" (Bermingham, *Landscape* 13)—of which Darcy has abundance. His gardener proudly informs the Gardiners that Darcy's property is "ten miles round" (Austen 253), which means that Darcy owns somewhere between four and five thousand acres (Greene 16). As Austen's description makes clear, Pemberley's gardens do not consist of ornamental trees, topiary, or flower beds, but rather of lawn sweeping up to the building itself, a fine wood, and a stream. The Davies production follows Austen in focusing on land, trees, and water in its shots of Pemberley; there is one brief scene of Elizabeth strolling through a more formal garden, laid out beside the house behind a high brick wall, but the garden consists of grasses, shrubs, and trees rather than flowers. The land itself provides the visual interest at Pemberley. Pemberley's grounds bear the unmistakable imprint of Capability Brown, whose improvements at Chatsworth bear a remarkable similarity to Darcy's improvements at Pemberley: "[Brown] widened the river and contrived so to raise its level as to bring it into his picture.... He planted the trees on the rising ground above the cascade and across the river, and laid out a new drive" (Hyams 219). Austen was clearly familiar with his work when she wrote *Pride and Prejudice*, since she mentions by name three of the houses whose gardens he improved: Chatsworth, Blenheim, and Warwick Castle. Brown was famous for using elements such as "serpentine waters, belts and clumps of trees, [and] smooth lawns right up to the house walls" (Hunt 151) in his designs; Brown's trademark touches in using the land itself as ornament aptly describe Darcy's improvements at Pemberley.

Simon Langton, the director of the 1995 version of *Pride and Prejudice*, chooses, not surprisingly, to linger lovingly at Pemberley. We see Pemberley from a distance and up close; we walk along its stream and through its trees; we go inside to gaze in awe at the Great Staircase and the Picture Gallery; we see its inner courtyards and outer staircases. As if this were not enough, Langton improvises an ornamental pond, some distance from the stream, beside which a hot and sweaty Darcy, just arrived on horseback from London, strips off most of his clothing to take a swim. How could Elizabeth, the model middle-class Picturesque tourist, help falling in love with all this? As she says rapturously when she and her uncle and aunt first spy Pemberley through the trees, "I don't think I've ever seen a place so happily situated. I like it very well indeed."

According to Carole Fabricant, great houses and grounds like Pemberley were calculated to inspire desire in their spectators. Landscape painting, tourist guides, and domestic tourism worked in conjunction to render "pieces of privately owned land accessible—and in a vicarious sense possessable— by their often middle-class audience" (Fabricant, "Literature" 259). The visual consumption of the houses and lands of the aristocracy in which the middle classes indulged themselves was akin to symbolic ownership; while the vast riches of Blenheim or Chatsworth would never (except in novels) be theirs, the middle classes could enjoy the pleasure grounds, tour the house, talk to the housekeeper, and take home a little piece of the great house in the form of a guidebook or engraving. Domestic tourism and the opening of great houses to the public coincide with the rise of the middle class as an economic and political force in British society; ideologically, domestic tourism bolstered the power of the aristocracy by calling attention to the disparity between the classes through the display of ancestral riches. Fabricant theorizes domestic tourism did, however, possess subversive potential "by virtue of exposing these creations to the hungry, perhaps covetous or resentful gaze of others, thereby possibly fostering, in spite of its official agenda, feelings of dispossession and alienation" (Fabricant, "Literature," 271–72).

Elizabeth herself is not unaware of the class tensions that underscore her visit to Pemberley. Darcy's class consciousness prevented him from dancing with her, a gentleman's daughter, at the Assembly Ball in Hertfordshire; how can she help believing that he will shun an acquaintance with her uncle, a tradesman with an unfashionable London address? At Pemberley, however, Darcy has an opportunity to shine as landlord, brother, master, to display his good taste and breeding, to show Elizabeth that her rejection of his proposal has influenced him to change, to become more open and less arrogant. Austen demonstrates Darcy's willingness to please through his treatment of the Gardiners. The makers of the 1995 film show him, instead, asking Elizabeth eagerly if she approves of his house. They downplay Elizabeth's attraction to his possessions by giving most of Austen's lines about the beauty of Pemberley's surroundings to the Gardiners. The filmmakers shy away from presenting Elizabeth at Pemberley as Austen presents her, consuming the view from Darcy's window with "something like regret" (Austen 246) for having rejected his proposal. The bond between Elizabeth and Darcy is forged not through her admiration for his possessions but through their mutual love of the wild and untamed landscape surrounding Pemberley. The filmmakers' focus throughout the film on landscape and fine views and, particularly, on depicting Elizabeth as part of the landscape, reaches its culmination in the Pemberley episodes, which are filmed as the apotheosis of landscape imagery. Depicting Elizabeth so exclusively within the landscape makes it seem natural for her to become mistress of what is, in the film, the most beautiful of many landscapes. The filmmakers reinscribe Elizabeth's desire for Pemberley into the viewer's desire to see Elizabeth at Pemberley.

The Davies production follows Austen in using the Pemberley episodes to focus Elizabeth's attention on a different side of Darcy, to correct her prejudice, and to counteract her dislike of Darcy. Elizabeth's appreciation of Pemberley's landscape is crucial to the development of her love for its owner: closure depends on Elizabeth's mental absorption in Darcy's landscape, which prefigures her physical absorption as mistress of the estate. Because the Pemberley chapters provide such richly suggestive visual material for filmmakers, especially for filmmakers trying to sell us a version of "OLD

ENGLAND," it comes as a surprise that the makers of the 1940 film choose to dispense with Elizabeth's domestic tour and her visit to Pemberley. The financial exigencies of Hollywood filmmaking are partly to blame for this: unlike the 1995 film, Huxley/Murfin's *Pride and Prejudice* was filmed inside a studio with backdrops representing gardens and houses. More important, however, is Huxley and Murfin's conception of Austen's novel, which differs significantly from Davies's conception in the BBC production. The 1940 *Pride and Prejudice*, more than the 1995 television film, reduces the novel to the pure "linear narrative" (Axelrod 205) of the love story between Darcy and Elizabeth. In Huxley and Murfin's rewrite of Austen's story, the Pemberley episodes are not necessary for closure. Elizabeth's prejudice against Darcy has been overcome long before the Pemberley chapters, as we realize shortly after the proposal scene, when Darcy arrives at Longbourn in person to acquaint her with Wickham's true character. After he leaves, she gazes out the window and wonders aloud, "Will he ever ride back?" The melodrama and sentimentality inherent in such a line indicate the nature of many of Huxley and Murfin's revisions.

Note

2. Donald Greene argues in his provocative article, "The Original of Pemberley" for an identification of Pemberley as Chatsworth, ancestral home of the dukes of Devonshire. He compares Austen's description of Pemberley's grounds with a contemporary guidebook describing the grounds of Chatsworth and finds remarkable similarities. Comparison of the houses is complicated by Austen's minimalist description: both have great staircases, impressive libraries, and picture galleries, as do many other great houses. It would be useful to compare Austen's description with eighteenth-century guidebooks to which she would have had access.

DONALD GRAY ON MONEY

It is very difficult to compute contemporary equivalents of the sums of money named in Jane Austen's novels. One commentator uses a factor of 33 to estimate that Mr. Bennet's annual income of £2,000 is worth about $66,000 in 1988 US dollars. Darcy's income by the same calculation is over $330,000, and Bingley's is about $165,000.[1] Another commentator uses a multiplier of 70 to 80 to suggest that Mr. Bennet's income is $165,000 in 1989 US dollars, and Darcy's is $800,000—about the sum, Mr. Bennet guesses, Darcy spent to bribe Wickham to marry Lydia ("Wickham's a fool, if he takes her with a farthing less than ten thousand pounds").[2] Mary Mogford, figuring that Darcy's income is 300 times that of the per capita income of Britain in 1810, multiplies the per capita income of the US in 1989 by that number to give him an annual income of over six million US dollars.[3]

Even were these calculations consistent with one another, they cannot take into account the difference in purchasing power in a time when labor was cheap, income taxes low, and landowners like Darcy and Mr. Bennet could partially supply their households from their own farms. (Mr. Bennet's daughters sometimes cannot use the horses because they are required for farmwork.) A more accurate measure of the economic status of characters in *Pride and Prejudice* is a comparison of the incomes Austen ascribes to them and the actual incomes of some of her contemporaries. In 1810 the nominal annual income of agricultural workers was £42, of skilled laborers between £55 and £90, of clerks £178, of clergymen £283, and of lawyers £447.[4] David Spring in an essay reprinted in this volume suggests that the income of a large merchant (perhaps such as Mr. Gardiner) was about that of a member of the "modest gentry," or pseudo-gentry, such as Mr. Bennet (see pp. 396f).

The income of the Austen family, early and late, was less than that of merchants and holders, however temporary, of estates like Mr. Bennet's. Like most other clergymen, Jane Austen's father derived his income from tithes levied on his parishioners and from the profits of farming the "glebe," a section of land set aside for the benefit of the church.[5] Mr. Austen's income from both sources at the beginning of his career was perhaps £200 a year from tithes and additional money from the lease on a nearby farm.[6] During her childhood he still needed to supplement his income by taking in pupils in the parsonage. But at the time of his retirement Jane Austen wrote in one of her letters, "I do not despair of [his] getting nearly six hundred a year" from his interest in his livings.[7]

Upon his death in 1805, however, this interest lapsed. His wife and two unmarried daughters were left with an annual income of a little over £200. Jane Austen's brothers agreed to contributions that doubled that sum.[8] After living for three years in Southampton—during one of which Austen recorded her personal expenses for the year as £50[9]—they were given the use of the cottage at Chawton. While she was resuming her work as a novelist and revising the novel in which Elizabeth Bennet becomes mistress of Pemberley, Jane Austen was settling in, with a maid, a manservant, a cook who was paid a little over £8 a year, and a new piano that cost about £30 (Tomalin 207; Nokes 346), to spend the rest of her life in a household managed on an annual income of about £460.[10]

Jane Austen's earnings from her writing have a place in these comparisons. During her lifetime Austen made less than £700 from her novels (Honan 393). She sold the copyright of *Pride and Prejudice* outright for £110 and made no more money from the sales of what even during her lifetime proved to be her most popular novel. All her other novels were published on commission, which meant that she was responsible for losses as well as eligible for profits after the publisher subtracted his costs and commission. She received £140 from the sales of the first edition of *Sense and Sensibility* (1811), the first of her novels to be published, and at least £60 from a second edition. The sales of the first edition of *Mansfield Park* earned her perhaps £320, and she wondered whether to risk a second edition: "People are more ready to borrow & praise, than to buy—which I cannot wonder at;—but tho' I like praise as well as anybody, I like what Edward calls *Pewter* too" (*Letters*, 30 Nov. 1814, 287). She did agree to a second edition, but in a memorandum on her earnings as a writer she notes that in 1816 the edition still posted a loss in her account at her publisher of nearly £200, which reduced her earnings on the sales of *Emma* (1816) to less than £40 (Honan 393). (Eventually the second edition of *Mansfield Park* made a profit, although not until after Austen's death.) The sales of *Persuasion* and *Northanger Abbey*, published posthumously in 1818, returned about £500 to her sister Cassandra (Tomalin 272). In 1832 Cassandra (who inherited Austen's copyrights) and one of her brothers sold the copyrights of all the novels except *Pride and Prejudice* (which they did not own) for £210 (Honan 320). In sum, in twenty years Jane Austen's writing brought her and her family less than £1,500, undoubtedly a welcome supplement to the discretionary incomes of two women who principally depended for support on their mother and brothers, but less than the annual income Austen imagined for Mr. Bennet.

As I have in the preceding paragraph, Austen typically states the wealth of women in lump sums, the wealth of men as annual income. The meaning of a woman's money is not that its income will support her, although at a 4 percent annual return Miss Darcy's £30,000 (Volume II, Chapter XII) and even Miss King's £10,000 (II, IV) would keep a single woman comfortably. (As Mr. Collins makes clear, that is not true of the £1,000 Elizabeth will inherit from her mother [I: XIX].) Rather, its meaning is that on her marriage a woman's money will pass as capital to her husband.[11] Having been one of the reasons for her desirability, her money will become one of the sources of the income by which his economic status is measured.

Notes

1. James Heldman, "How Wealthy Is Mr. Darcy, Really." *Persuasions* 12 (1990): 38–49.

2. Edward Copeland, "The Economic Realities of Jane Austen's Day," in Approaches to Teaching Jane Austen's *"Pride and Prejudice,"* ed. Marcia McClintock Folsom (New York, 1993) 33–45. See also Copeland's essay, "Money," in The *Cambridge* Companion to Jane Austen, ed. Edward Copeland and Juliet McMaster (Cambridge and New York, 1997) 131–48.

3. "Darcy's Wealth: An Addendum," *Persuasions* 13 (1991): 49.

4. B.R. Mitchell, *British Historical Statistics* (New York: Cambridge University Press, 1988) 153.

5. See Irene Collins, *Jane Austen and the Clergy* (London and Rio Grande, OH: Hambledon, 1993) 49–60.

6. Claire Tomalin, *Jane Austen: A Life* (London: Peters, Frances and Dunlop; New York: Alfred A. Knopf, 1997) 7.

7. *Jane Austen's Letters*, ed. Deirdre Le Faye (Oxford and New York: Oxford University Press, 1995) 3–5 Jan. 1801, 69.

8. David Nokes, *Jane Austen: A Life* (London: Fourth Estate; New York: Farrar, Straus, and Giroux, 1997) 274–75.

9. Nokes, 310; Park Honan, Jane Austen: Her Life (New York: St. Martin's Press, 1987) 244–45.

10. John Halperin, *The Life of Jane Austen* (Baltimore: John Hopkins University Press; Brighton: Harvester Press, 1984) 145.

11. Judith Lowder Newton, Women, Power, *Subversion* (Athens: University of Georgia Press, 1981) 56; Mary Evans, *Jane Austen and the State* (London and New York: Tavistock, 1987) 20–21.

EFRAHT MARGULIET ON ELIZABETH'S PETTICOAT

According to Roland Barthes, "The description of a garment may be the site of rhetorical connotation" (*Fashion* 235–36).[1] This paper addresses a certain reference to dress and fashion in *Pride and Prejudice* that serves as an indirect presentation of character-traits; that is, a reference that does not name or describe explicitly the traits of a character but rather displays and exemplifies them, "leaving to the reader the task of inferring the [qualities it implies]" (Rimmon–Kenan 59–61).

The discussion regarding Lizzy's garments and appearance after she arrives at Netherfield to visit her ill sister Jane functions as such a character-indicator. It affects the characterization not only of Elizabeth, but also of Miss Bingley and Mrs. Hurst. One may assume that Jane Austen's contemporary reader was well acquainted with the "cultural code" to which she was referring, and was thus able to grasp immediately the innuendoes of the Bingley sisters' parley (*S/Z* 20).[2] However, the modern reader who is not thoroughly aware of the cultural backdrop of Austen's writing might miss its undertones. I shall examine the implications of Caroline and

Louisa's focus on Elizabeth's soiled petticoat and show how, while aiming to reinforce their overt disparagement of the visitor, the speakers inadvertently expose themselves.

On the first evening Elizabeth spends at Netherfield, she leaves the ladies and returns to her sister's bedside:

> Miss Bingley began abusing her as soon as she was out of the room. Her manners were pronounced to be very bad indeed, a mixture of pride and impertinence; she had no conversation, no stile [sic], no taste, no beauty. Mrs. Hurst thought the same, and added,
>
> "She has nothing, in short, to recommend her, but being an excellent walker. I shall never forget her appearance this morning. She really looked almost wild."
>
> "She did indeed, Louisa. I could hardly keep my countenance. Very nonsensical to come at all! Why must *she* be scampering about the country, because her sister had a cold? Her hair, so untidy, so blowsy!"
>
> "Yes, and her **petticoat**; I hope you saw her **petticoat**, six inches deep in mud, I am absolutely certain; and the gown which had been let down to hide it, not doing its office."
>
> "Your picture may be very exact, Louisa," said Bingley; "but ... I thought Miss Elizabeth Bennet looked remarkably well.... Her dirty **petticoat** quite escaped my notice."
>
> "*You* observed it, Mr. Darcy, I am sure," said Miss Bingley; "and I am inclined to think that you would not wish to see *your sister* make such an exhibition."
>
> "Certainly not."
>
> (*P&P* 35–36; italics in text, boldface mine)

Barthes points out that "every intransitive (unproductive) description founds the possibility of a certain poetics"; "by describing a material object, if it is not to construct it or to use it, we are led to link the qualities of its matter to a second meaning, to be signified through the notable which we attribute to it" (*Fashion* 235–36). The "second meaning" invoked by Caroline's and Louisa's description of Lizzy's appearance is that of gross impropriety verging on immodesty. Their censure of Elizabeth, using her appearance as ammunition, is ironized by the text, ultimately reflecting on the soiled and superficial nature of their own ostensible gentility rather than on Elizabeth's honor.

It is significant that the sisters decide to concentrate on the petticoat and to prolong the discussion of it. The choice of the petticoat is a barely veiled attack on Elizabeth's feminine honor and thus extends the criticism levelled at her into the realms of both sexuality and morality. As Barthes claims, "Language ... conveys a choice and imposes it, it requires the perception of this dress to stop here (i.e., neither before nor beyond), it arrests the level of reading at its fabric, at its belt, at the accessory which adorns it. Thus, every written word has a function of authority insofar as it chooses" (*Fashion* 13). Barthes's example of a specific dress demonstrates one fundamental function of "written clothing" (*Fashion* 4), which is suggested by the discourse of Caroline and Louisa. The sisters refer to Elizabeth's petticoat not only to ground their explicit slander but to expand it by implication.

(...)

Therefore, the "notable" that Jane Austen's readers would have attributed to the dirty petticoat touches upon sexual indecency (*Fashion* 235). The sisters' rather general remark on Elizabeth's being "almost wild" is thus anchored in a very specific context.[5] Furthermore, the reference to Elizabeth's unsuccessful effort to "hide" the muddy petticoat by letting down her gown is meant to indicate that she does not possess even the finesse required to conceal so gross an impropriety.

(...)

The Bingley sisters' parley gave Jane Austen's contemporary reader, who was well aware of its connotations of indecency, an important indication of the maliciously tainted minds of the sisters rather than a reliable judgment of the heroine.

Because the explicit references to Lizzy's character do not "proceed from the most authoritative voice[s] in the text" (Rimmon-Kenan 60), the reader accepts at face value neither the sisters' slander nor its abusive implications. However, since what a "character says about another may characterize not only the one spoken about but also the one who speaks" (Rimmon-Kenan 64), the episode confirms Elizabeth's initial disapproval of Miss Bingley and Mrs. Hurst. Eager to debase Elizabeth and, by association, to degrade Jane, the sisters unwittingly expose their own coarseness. Furthermore, in their insistence on dwelling on the delicate subject of the petticoat, Louisa and Caroline reveal how threatened they are by the growing attention their brother and Darcy pay to the Bennet sisters.

Since Jane Austen uses descriptive details economically, the attentive reader can gain a more comprehensive understanding of her works by exploring the cultural code underlying such details. By noting the socio-cultural significance of the petticoat at the time *Pride and Prejudice* was written we are able not only to understand why the Bingley sisters insistently refer to it, but also to pick up on the ironic undertone of the dialogue which foreshadows the text's final rejection of mock propriety, propriety that has everything to do with appearances and nothing to do with true gentility.

Notes

1. Although Barthes discusses texts that relate to photographed clothing in fashion magazines, many of his assertions are applicable to literary texts that relate to what he calls "imagined" garments, cf. p. 6.

2. The cultural code, according to Barthes, is comprised of a text's "references to a science or a body of knowledge" existing outside itself thus creating a context or a set of meanings for the reader to decipher.

5. In this context the "exhibition" that Elizabeth makes of herself ought to be distinguished from Mary's "exhibiting" at the Netherfield ball (36, 101). Mary's performance merely exposes her poor social skills and her inferior singing and playing while Elizabeth's dirty petticoat presumably impinges on her morals and sexual decency.

Works by Jane Austen

Austen's *Juvenilia*:
Volume I, written between 1787 and 1790.
Volume II, written between 1790 and 1792.
   includes: *Love and Freindship* [sic]
               The History of England
Volume III, written between 1792 and 1793.

Sense and Sensibility, 1811.

Pride and Prejudice, 1813.

Mansfield Park, 1814.

Emma, 1815.

Northanger Abbey, 1817.

Persuasion, 1817.

The Watsons, fragment written 1803–1805; published 1871.

Sanditon, unfinished at her death.

Annotated Bibliography

Austen-Leigh, William, and Richard Arthur Austen-Leigh. *Jane Austen: A Family Record*. Revised and Enlarged by Deirdre Le Faye. Boston: G.K. Hall & Co., 1989.

This collection, originally compiled in 1913 by Richard Austen-Leigh and William Austen-Leigh includes a vast variety of letters and anecdotes from the Austen family. In this edition, it is supplemented with additional information collected by the family, a detailed chronology of Austen's life, family pedigree charts, and a very personal and detailed biography of the author.

Batey, Mavis. *Jane Austen and the English Landscape*. London: Barn Elms Publishing, 1996.

Illustrated with full-color plates, this book offers images of the time period and landscapes that inspired Jane Austen. There are watercolor images from Austen's time, portraying vibrant landscapes and intimate domestic scenes, illustration plates from contemporary novels, and depictions of the architecture of English estates. The images provide context for understanding Austen's world.

Bloom, Harold. *Jane Austen's Pride and Prejudice*. New York: Chelsea House Publishers, 1987.

Provides a selection of important critical articles on *Pride and Prejudice* published between 1973 and 1983, offering a variety of useful perspectives. The essays are arranged chronologically, giving a sense of the evolving themes of interest to critics.

Butler, Marilyn. *Jane Austen and the War of Ideas*. Oxford: Oxford University Press, 1987.

Butler reads the novel as a parable in which Elizabeth is able to join the aristocracy by giving up her initial protest to it. She reads the novel in the context of other, more directly political writers of the period, including William Godwin, Robert Bage, and Maria Edgeworth.

Chapman, R.W., editor *Jane Austen's Letters to her Sister Cassandra and Others*, Second edition. London, 1952.

Austen wrote a large number of letters throughout her lifetime, many of which have been preserved, and provide great insights to her life and writing. Chapman's edition is generally considered authoritative; Chapman also edited the standard edition of Jane Austen's works, first published in 1923.

Gay, Penny. *Jane Austen and the Theatre*. Cambridge: Cambridge University Press, 2002.

In Austen's early life, she wrote and performed short plays for her family; her lifelong interest in the theater is portrayed in Gay's work, including a chapter on each of Austen's novels and their connections to various genres of theater that existed in Austen's time.

Gilbert, Sandra M. and Susan Gubar. *The Madwoman in the Attic: The Woman Writer and the 19th-Century Literary Imagination*. New Haven: Yale University Press, 1979.

For a ground-breaking early feminist reading of Jane Austen, see Part II, "Inside the House of Fiction: Jane Austen's Tenants of Possibility," of this seminal work.

Gilson, David. *A Bibliography of Jane Austen*. Oxford: Oxford University Press, 1982.

This comprehensive bibliography is usually considered the standard bibliography, containing a complete list of secondary materials published until 1978.

Gorman, Anita G. *The Body in Illness and Health: Themes and Images in Jane Austen*. New York: Peter Lang, 1993.

This is a study of the way Austen portrays characters' bodies as healthy or ill, particularly characters' hypochondria. It studies these themes throughout her work, including some pieces on *Pride and Prejudice*.

Grey, J. David, editor. *The Jane Austen Companion*. New York: Macmillan Publishing, 1988.

This is a collection of a wide array of short essays, including surveys of different periods of Austen criticism. It also includes a "Dictionary of Austen's Life and Works," assembled by H. Abigail Bok.

Gross, Gloria Sybil. *In a Fast Coach with a Pretty Woman: Jane Austen and Samuel Johnson*. New York: AMS Press, 2002.

Considers her juvenilia and her major novels in light of Austen's admiration of the life and works of Samuel Johnson.

Honan, Park. *Jane Austen: Her Life*. New York: Ballantine Books, 1989.

Using Austen family manuscripts, Honan's biography focuses on Austen's personal and family life, as well as her writing during her time at Chawton.

Hughes-Hallett, Penelope. *My Dear Cassandra: The Letters of Jane Austen*. New York: Clarkson Potter Publishers, 1990.

An illustrated collection of letters between Jane and her sister, Cassandra. Offers reproductions of period illustrations and fashion plates, and portraits of the Austen family. The text of letters from every period of Austen's life is enhanced by these images, which provide the reader with a visual sense of Austen's time.

McMaster, Juliet. *Jane Austen the Novelist: Essays Past and Present*. New York: St. Martin's Press, 1996.

This is an excellent collection of essays covering a variety of Austen's works by a noted Austen scholar.

Mooneyham, Laura G. *Romance, Language, and Education in Jane Austen's Novels*. New York: St. Martin's Press, 1988.

One chapter focuses on *Pride and Prejudice*, the others on each of her other novels. The study observes the speech patterns and language development (or lack thereof) of various characters to show their education and sensibility.

Morris, Ivor. *Mr. Collins Considered*. London: Routledge & Kegan Paul, 1987.

Morris's work focuses on the rather amusing character of Mr. Collins, evaluating him on various areas, including wealth, station, and romance. Collins is portrayed as a comic figure, and his characterization is flat; however, Ivor explores his role in the novel and the oeuvre of Austen in depth.

Poplawski, Paul. *A Jane Austen Encyclopedia*. Westport, Connecticut: Greenwood Press, 1998.

Provides a chronology of Austen's life, and a literary chronology that places Austen's work in the context of her predecessors and contemporaries. The encyclopedia arranges short entries alphabetically, including a listing for each character, and summaries of her novels and various juvenilia. It also provides several bibliographies, including a chronological summary of Austen criticism.

Seeber, Barbara K. *General Consent in Jane Austen: A Study of Dialogism*. Montreal: McGill-Queen's University, 2000.

Explores the ongoing debate about whether Austen's work is generally conformist or quietly subversive. She uses Mikhail Bakhtin's theories to explore the ways that Austen manages to be both, particularly in *Mansfield Park*, although all of her novels and some juvenilia are also considered.

Southam, B.C., Editor. *Jane Austen: The Critical Heritage. Revised Edition*. London: Routledge & Kegan Paul, 1986.

This is an essential history of the criticism of Austen, including original reviews of her novels. There are excerpts from letters, reviews, and commentaries discussing Austen through 1870.

Troost, Linda, and Sayre Greenfield, Editors. *Jane Austen in Hollywood. Second Edition*. Lexington: The University Press of Kentucky, 2001.

This is an excellent collection of essays on the film adaptations of Austen's novels. It explores how and why

Austen has enjoyed such cinematic popularity, and the kinds of changes that are made in adapting these novels to film. There are film stills from a number of the adaptations, as well as reviews and brief commentaries. There is a filmography of adaptations dating to the 1940s,

Tuite, Clara. *Romantic Austen: Sexual Politics and the Literary Canon*. Cambridge: Cambridge University Press, 2002.

This study considers Austen within the tradition of British Romanticism, reading Austen's juvenilia, *Sense and Sensibility*, *Mansfield Park*, and the uncompleted *Sandition*, to show her engagement with Romantic-era themes and political concerns. Tuite also provides a rereading of other twentieth-century scholarship on Austen.

Waldron, Mary. *Jane Austen and the Fiction of Her Time*. Cambridge: Cambridge University Press, 1999.

Waldron reads Austen as a radical innovator, who confronted the other popular novelists of her time, challenging them to transform their fiction. In her personal correspondence with her family, Austen frequently critiqued novels; this study examines how her own critique of the genre she wrote inflects her novel writing.

Contributors

HAROLD BLOOM is Sterling Professor of the Humanities at Yale University. He is the author of over 20 books, including *Shelley's Mythmaking* (1959), *The Visionary Company* (1961), *Blake's Apocalypse* (1963), *Yeats* (1970), *A Map of Misreading* (1975), *Kabbalah and Criticism* (1975), *Agon: Toward a Theory of Revisionism* (1982), *The American Religion* (1992), *The Western Canon* (1994), and *Omens of Millennium: The Gnosis of Angels, Dreams, and Resurrection* (1996). *The Anxiety of Influence* (1973) sets forth Professor Bloom's provocative theory of the literary relationships between the great writers and their predecessors. His most recent books include *Shakespeare: The Invention of the Human* (1998), a 1998 National Book Award finalist, *How to Read and Why* (2000), *Genius: A Mosaic of One Hundred Exemplary Creative Minds* (2002), and *Hamlet: Poem Unlimited* (2003). In 1999, Professor Bloom received the prestigious American Academy of Arts and Letters Gold Medal for Criticism, and in 2002 he received the Catalonia International Prize.

E.M. HALLIDAY, a professor at the University of North Carolina State College of Agriculture and Engineering, Raleigh, NC, also served as editor of *American Heritage*.

STUART TAVE is the William Rainey Harper Professor Emeritus in the College and the Department of English Language & Literature at the University of Chicago. A noted Austen scholar, and author of *Some Words of Jane Austen* (1973), he retired in 1993.

SANDRA M. GILBERT is Professor of English at the University of California, Davis. *The Madwoman in the Attic: The Woman Writer and the 19th-Century Literary Imagination* was a runner-up for both the Pulitzer Prize and the National Book Critics Circle Award. The two have collaborated on several projects, most recently the editing of the *Norton Anthology of Literature by Women: The Traditions in English* (1996).

SUSAN GUBAR is Distinguished Professor of English and Women's Studies at Indiana University, Bloomington. *The Madwoman in the Attic: The Woman Writer and the 19th-Century Literary Imagination* was a runner-up for both the Pulitzer Prize and the National Book Critics Circle Award. The two have collaborated on several projects, most recently the editing of the *Norton Anthology of Literature by Women: The Traditions in English* (1996).

TONY TANNER was Professor of English and American Literature at the University of Cambridge and a Fellow of King's College, Cambridge. He published numerous books, including *Jane Austen* (1986).

LAURA G. MOONEYHAM-WHITE is Professor of English at the University of Nebraska, Lincoln. She is the author of *Romance, Language, and Education in Jane Austen's Novels*.

ANITA G.GORMAN is Associate Professor of English at Slippery Rock University, where she teaches composition and British literature.

ANNE CRIPPEN RUDERMAN earned her Ph.D. at the University of Chicago. She has lectured in political science at Cornell University and Colgate University.

JULIET McMASTER is the co-editor of *The Cambridge Companion to Jane Austen* and *Jane Austen on Love* and the author of *Jane Austen the Novelist: Essays Past and Present*. She is a Professor of English the University of Alberta.

ALLISON THOMPSON is a writer, musician, dancer, and historian of the dance. Her most recent work is *Dancing Through Time: Western Social Dance in Literature, 1400–1918*.

H. ELIZABETH ELLINGTON worked on her Ph.D. at Brandeis and studies women writers of World War I. She earned her undergraduate degree at Vesalius College in Belgium, and her Masters at the University of New Hampshire.

DONALD GRAY is the editor of the Norton Critical Edition of Jane Austen's *Pride and Prejudice* (3rd edition, 2001).

EFRAHT MARGULIET received her degree in English in 2001 from the Hebrew University of Jerusalem. She is the editor of *Truman News*, the newsletter of the Harry S. Truman Research Institute for the Advancement of Peace at the Hebrew University.

Acknowledgments

"Narrative Perspective in *Pride and Prejudice*" by E.M. Halliday. From *Nineteenth Century Fiction*, Vol. 15, No. 1 (Jun., 1960), 65–71. Reprinted by permission.

"Affection and the Mortification of Elizabeth Bennet" by Stuart Tave. From *Some Words of Jane Austen*. Chicago: U of Chicago P, 1973. 131, 138–139. Reprinted by permission.

Excerpts from *The Madwoman in the Attic: The Woman Writer and the 19th-Century Literary Imagination* by Sandra M. Gilbert and Susan Gubar. New Haven: Yale University Press, 1979. 154–155, 157. Reprinted by permission.

"Knowledge and Opinion: *Pride and Prejudice*" by Tony Tanner. From *Jane Austen*. London: Macmillan, 1986. 132–134. Reprinted by permission.

"*Pride and Prejudice:* Toward a Common Language" by Laura G. Mooneyham. From *Romance, Language, and Education in Jane Austen's Novels*. New York: St. Martin's Press, 1988. 45–47. Reprinted by permission.

"Pictures of Health: The Appearance of Characters Major and Minor" by Anita G. Gorman. From *The Body in Illness and Health: Themes and Images in Jane Austen*. New York: Peter Lang, 1993. 172–175. Reprinted by permission.

"Proper Pride and Religious Virtue" by Anne Crippen Ruderman. From *The Pleasures of Virtue: Political Thought in the Novels of Jane Austen*. Lanham, Maryland: Rowman & Littlefield Publishers, Inc., 1995. 101–104. Reprinted by Permission.

"'Acting By Design' in *Pride and Prejudice*" by Juliet McMaster. From *Jane Austen the Novelist: Essays Past and Present*. New York: St. Martin's Press, 1996. 80–85. Reprinted by permission.

"The Felicities of Rapid Motion: Jane Austen in the Ballroom" by Allison Thompson. From *Persuasions On-Line*. Vol. 21, No. 1. Winter 2000. Reprinted by permission.

"'A Correct Taste in Landscape' Pemberley as Fetish and Commodity" by H. Elisabeth Ellington. From *Jane Austen in Hollywood*, *Second Edition* Troost, Linda, and Sayre Greenfield, Editors.. Lexington: The University Press of Kentucky, 2001. 98–103. Reprinted by permission.

"A Note on Money" by Donald Gray. From *Pride and Prejudice: An Authoritative Text Backgrounds and Sources Criticism*, *Third Edition*. Ed. Donald Gray. New York: W.W. Norton & Company, 2001. 403–405. Reprinted by permission.

"On Pettiness and Petticoats: The Significance of the Petticoat in *Pride and Prejudice*" by Efraht Marguliet. From *Persuasions On-Line*. Vol. 23, No. 1. Winter 2002. Reprinted by permission.

Index

Characters are indexed under their last names.

A

"Affection." *See* Love
Anne (*Persuasion*), 69, 71
As You Like It (Shakespeare), 7–8
Austen, Cassandra, 10–11, 101
Austen, Jane
  biographical sketch, 10–12
  income of, 13, 99–101
Austen, Jane, style of
  capitulation in, 68
  characterization in, 7, 102–105
  compared to Shakespeare, 7–9
  conduct vs. morality, 65, 76–77
  descriptions of Elizabeth, 71–73
  irony, 8, 59
  narrative voice of, 7–8, 59–62
  portrayal of women, 27–28, 63–65
  relationships in novels, 68–69
Austen, Jane, works of, 11–12, 106.
  See also *Pride and Prejudice*
Elinor and Marianne, 13
Emma, 11, 68, 69, 72, 101
First Impressions, 13
A History of England by a partial, prejudiced and ignorant Historian, 10
juvenilia, 10, 13, 80
Love and Freindship, 10, 80
Mansfield Park, 11, 68, 69, 100, 101
Northanger Abbey, 11, 13, 63, 68, 69
Persuasion, 11, 68, 69, 101
Sandition, 11
Sense and Sensibility, 11, 13, 69, 100
Susan, 13

B

Balls and dancing, 22–24, 29–30, 84–89
Banfield, Ann, 89
Barthes, Roland, 102–105
Bennet, Elizabeth (character)
  Austen on, 14
  becomes focus of story, 59–60
  character of, 7–8, 23
  character sketch, 17
  compared to Rosalind, 7–8
  contrasted with Jane, 33–34, 65
  Darcy proposes, 38, 55
  descriptions of, 71–73
  emotional made intellectual by, 82
  father's influence on, 80–85
  as heroine, 68–71
  manners of, 74–75
  marriage of, 57, 59
  misjudgments of, 40, 43–44, 63, 70, 83
  visits Charlotte, 35–36
  warms to Darcy, 47, 50, 62–63
  wit of, 7, 64, 69–70, 80–83
Bennet, Jane (character)
  character of, 23
  character sketch, 17
  contrasted with Elizabeth, 33–34, 65
  illness at Netherfield, 25–26, 60, 79, 102–105
  letters to Elizabeth, 34, 46
  London visit, 34
  marriage of, 57, 59
  Mr. Bingley proposes, 53
Bennet, Catherine (character), 18, 41, 42, 43, 48
Bennet, Lydia (character)
  character sketch, 18
  elopement with Wickham, 46–51, 62–63, 66

117